SpringerBriefs in Ethics

Springer Briefs in Ethics envisions a series of short publications in areas such as business ethics, bioethics, science and engineering ethics, food and agricultural ethics, environmental ethics, human rights and the like. The intention is to present concise summaries of cutting-edge research and practical applications across a wide spectrum.

Springer Briefs in Ethics are seen as complementing monographs and journal articles with compact volumes of 50 to 125 pages, covering a wide range of content from professional to academic. Typical topics might include:

- Timely reports on state-of-the art analytical techniques
- A bridge between new research results, as published in journal articles, and a contextual literature review
- A snapshot of a hot or emerging topic
- In-depth case studies or clinical examples
- Presentations of core concepts that students must understand in order to make independent contributions

Onno Bouwmeester

Business Ethics and Critical Consultant Jokes

New Research Methods to Study Ethical Transgressions

Onno Bouwmeester
Department of Management
and Organization
Vrije Universiteit Amsterdam
Amsterdam, The Netherlands

ISSN 2211-8101　　　　　　　ISSN 2211-811X　(electronic)
SpringerBriefs in Ethics
ISBN 978-3-031-10200-4　　　ISBN 978-3-031-10201-1　(eBook)
https://doi.org/10.1007/978-3-031-10201-1

© The Author(s) 2022. This book is an open access publication.
Open Access This book is licensed under the terms of the Creative Commons Attribution 4.0 International License (http://creativecommons.org/licenses/by/4.0/), which permits use, sharing, adaptation, distribution and reproduction in any medium or format, as long as you give appropriate credit to the original author(s) and the source, provide a link to the Creative Commons license and indicate if changes were made.

The images or other third party material in this book are included in the book's Creative Commons license, unless indicated otherwise in a credit line to the material. If material is not included in the book's Creative Commons license and your intended use is not permitted by statutory regulation or exceeds the permitted use, you will need to obtain permission directly from the copyright holder.

The use of general descriptive names, registered names, trademarks, service marks, etc. in this publication does not imply, even in the absence of a specific statement, that such names are exempt from the relevant protective laws and regulations and therefore free for general use.

The publisher, the authors, and the editors are safe to assume that the advice and information in this book are believed to be true and accurate at the date of publication. Neither the publisher nor the authors or the editors give a warranty, expressed or implied, with respect to the material contained herein or for any errors or omissions that may have been made. The publisher remains neutral with regard to jurisdictional claims in published maps and institutional affiliations.

This Springer imprint is published by the registered company Springer Nature Switzerland AG
The registered company address is: Gewerbestrasse 11, 6330 Cham, Switzerland

Preface

Laughing is part of human life. We start laughing quite early in life and we continue to do so. It can help us to cope with life, to better communicate with adolescents, or to create atmosphere among friends. It also helps to connect to people you like, and to disconnect with what you dislike. We can laugh about our own failures, as well as about what others do wrong. We can laugh to criticize as well as to express our sympathy, or both. Laughing can carry ambiguity, and so does joking. Maybe this ambiguity explains why jokes have been very absent in research methods.

The study of ethics is one of the domains of philosophy. While philosophy is considered the mother of science, with links to all scientific disciplines, it has no own empirical research tradition. It can reflect on empirical science, but mainly builds on ideas. While this makes philosophy rather detached from empirics, it still aims to be relevant to life, and this applies to ethics in particular. While logic, deduction, and theorizing might be the preferred methods in philosophy, when it comes to ethics or aesthetics generic logics meet their limits. General moral rules never always apply. We should not kill. But there are still cases where we feel it is justified to do so. We often make exceptions to moral rules, based on ethical deliberation, because we feel these should not apply in some cases. That is also why we need judges next to laws, and why ethics cannot be a rule book. It is why ethical norms are debated and also change over time, and, why sometimes, violating moral rules or expectations can be funny.

Jokes do exactly this: they play with violating norms. Rule-based expectations can be linked to ethics as well as to aesthetics and more. 'What is worse than one soprano? Two sopranos'. Or 'how do you recognize a consultant? He first borrows your watch and then tells you the time'. Reasonable moral or aesthetic expectations are broken in these cases. We expect the consultant to have knowledge and expertise, and the soprano to have skill and splendour, but we recognize they do not always have. As ethics should be able to study both the ethical rules, principles and virtues as well as exceptions and violations, its method cannot be only theoretical. It needs case based, empirical inquiry as well, and good empirical methods are currently underdeveloped in ethics.

This book seeks to show how interpreting jokes can be relevant to the empirical study of business ethics. By connecting traditional social science methods to various uses of jokes, this study offers new methods relevant to the field of business ethics. The jokes-based research methods are demonstrated for the ethics of management consultants, but it could have been another profession as well. Still, consultants provide a good case, because there are many business jokes on consultants who break written and unwritten rules, and the jokes show how. Integrating business jokes in research methods can offer new, rich insights into common moral transgressions, as well as into violated values, virtues and principles in the business context.

Amsterdam, The Netherlands   Onno Bouwmeester

Acknowledgements

Some material I build on in the book has been published before. If this is the case, an acknowledgement has been made at the end of the chapter where the material is used. One of the used articles I wrote together with Jelmer Stiekema, and another one with Tessa Kok. Both were students in the master program management consulting, and they wanted to work with jokes-based research methods in their master thesis projects. They have helped me to test and refine two methods, and I have enjoyed these collaborations very much. I also have to mention Oscar Haffmans who was first in collecting consulting jokes for his master thesis to do a content analysis. I build on this initial collection of jokes in the jokes-based articles to come. This is how the seeds of this book idea were planted.

Ruben van Werven was the first to give a friendly review on the current book. He is my co-author in articles not related to this book project. Ruben's feedback helped me to give better answers on the practical questions related to each of the methods, and to show how these methods have added value compared to more traditional research approaches. My colleague in business ethics Rebecca Ruehle was second to give a friendly review, and her comments helped me to better frame the book as a method book. Findings related to the context of application—consultants and their ethics—provide a secondary contribution, while the method contributions come first. She also made me aware of the different audiences I write for, being a former PhD student in business ethics. For a PhD student it is practical to have all information on one method in the same chapter, which made me move all sections on reviewer comments from the last chapter to the main chapters. This will help any scholarly audience, from ethics to social science scholars, interested in the methods. Third to give a friendly review was Ard-Pieter de Man, a Dutch consultant, university professor and a direct colleague for more than ten years. His main suggestion was to better discuss what kind of research questions the different methods help to answer, and to better show the similarities between the four methods in terms of relevant validity conditions, which resulted in Table 6.2. Finally, two anonymous reviewers helped me the strengthen my argument. First by suggesting relevant references that support my ideas, and second by better addressing the audience of ethics scholars of whom many will be philosophers without any experience in empirical research methods, and maybe also without a motive to build such experience. I hope to provide them with a motive.

While the book is finished now, the methods certainly are not. I can imagine that those who are going to apply these methods, find ways to improve them further, how to better report them, and how to generate new empirical insights that help us understand ethics better, as well as the cases in which we are challenged.

Contents

1 **Introduction of Jokes-Based Research Methods** 1
   1.1 Traditional Studies of Ethical Transgressions in Business 1
      1.1.1 Journalists Reporting on Unethical Business Practices
           That Include Consultants 1
      1.1.2 Academic Studies on Consultants' Ethics and Their
           Methods 3
   1.2 Unethical Business Practices and Public Jokes 6
      1.2.1 Literature Studies and Ethics 6
      1.2.2 Humour Theories and Joking About Unethical
           Practices 8
      1.2.3 Jokes-Based Research Methods and Research Ethics 11
   1.3 Outline and Contributions 12
   References 14

2 **Jokes That Illustrate Unethical Business Behaviour** 21
   2.1 Introduction to a Jokes-Based Method of Illustration 21
   2.2 The Issue—Code Violations as Food for Jokes 22
   2.3 Application—Ten Business Ethical Transgressions Illustrated 24
      2.3.1 Illustration Method: How to Search and Select Jokes
           Illustrating the Top Ten 24
      2.3.2 Illustration Results: A Top Ten of Ethical
           Transgressions in Business Jokes 25
      2.3.3 Jokes-Based Illustrations and Their Contributions
           to Ethical Research Questions 38
   2.4 Possibilities and Limitations of Jokes as Illustrations 39
      2.4.1 Jokes Can Illustrate Common Unethical Business
           Behaviours 39
      2.4.2 Method Limitations of Using Jokes as Illustration
           of Ethical Transgressions 41
      2.4.3 Reviewer Perspectives on Jokes-Based Illustrations
           and Possible Responses 42

	2.4.4	Practical Tips for Searching Critical Business Jokes	43
	References	44

3 Critical Jokes and Moral Reflection in Interviews ... 47
3.1 Introduction to a Jokes-Based Interview Method ... 47
3.2 The Issue—Experiencing Overly Pressuring Leadership ... 48
3.3 Application—Open Interviews and Jokes Based Reflections ... 49
    3.3.1 Jokes-Based Interview Method: Start with Reflecting on Critical Business Jokes ... 49
    3.3.2 Interview Results Show Recognition, Nuancing, and Going Beyond the Cartoon ... 51
    3.3.3 Jokes-Based Interviews and Their Contribution to Ethical Research Questions ... 54
3.4 Possibilities and Limitations of Jokes-Based Interviews ... 55
    3.4.1 Critical Cartoons Stimulate Reflections on Business Ethical Transgressions ... 55
    3.4.2 Method Limitation of Jokes-Based Interviews ... 57
    3.4.3 Reviewer Perspectives on Jokes-Based Interviews and Possible Responses ... 58
References ... 59

4 Jokes-Based Survey Questions on Expert Virtues ... 61
4.1 Introduction to a Jokes-Based Survey Method ... 61
4.2 The Issue—Opinions on Consultants' Lack of Expertise ... 62
4.3 Application—Using Expertise Cartoons to Study Opinions ... 63
    4.3.1 Jokes-Based Survey Method: Rating Cartoons Next to Traditional Statements ... 63
    4.3.2 Survey Results: Cartoon-Based and Statement-Based Responses ... 66
    4.3.3 Jokes-Based Survey Method and Contributions to Ethical Research Questions ... 69
4.4 Possibilities and Limitations of a Jokes-Based Survey Method ... 70
    4.4.1 How to Make Use of Cartoon-Based Rating Questions in a Survey ... 70
    4.4.2 Method Limitations of Jokes-Based Rating Questions in a Survey ... 71
    4.4.3 Reviewer Perspectives on Jokes-Based Surveys and Possible Responses ... 72
References ... 73

5 Content Analysis of Critical Business Jokes ... 75
5.1 Introduction to a Jokes-Based Method of Content Analysis ... 75
5.2 The Issue—Using Consultant and Client Uncertainties ... 76
5.3 Application—Analysing a Sample of Critical Business Jokes ... 77
    5.3.1 Method of Jokes-Based Content Analysis: Sampling and Open Coding ... 77

		5.3.2	Results: Tactics Related to Client and Consultant Uncertainty	78
		5.3.3	Jokes-Based Content Analysis and Contributions to Ethical Research Questions	82
	5.4	Possibilities and Limitations of Jokes-Based Content Analysis		83
		5.4.1	Larger Samples of Jokes Provide Richer Accounts of Ethical Norm Violation	83
		5.4.2	Method Limitations of Jokes-Based Content Analysis	84
		5.4.3	Reviewer Perspectives on Jokes-Based Content Analysis and Possible Responses	85
	References			86
6	**Concluding Reflections on Jokes-Based Research Methods**			89
	6.1	Introduction		89
	6.2	Scope and Benefits of Jokes-Based Research Methods		90
		6.2.1	Use of Jokes as Illustration in Business Ethics Research	90
		6.2.2	Use of Jokes-Based Interviews in Business Ethics Research	91
		6.2.3	Use of Jokes-Based Surveys in Business Ethics Research	92
		6.2.4	Use of Jokes-Based Content Analysis in Business Ethics Research	93
	6.3	Validity of the Four Jokes-Based Research Methods		93
	6.4	Wider Applications of Jokes-Based Research Methods		96
		6.4.1	Using Jokes-Based Research Methods in Wider Contexts of Norm Violation	96
		6.4.2	Jokes-Based Research in Course Assignments	96
		6.4.3	Further Sources to Explore in Jokes-Based Research Methods	97
	6.5	Analytic and Normative Value of Jokes in Business Ethics		98
	References			100

About the Author

Onno Bouwmeester is associate professor in management consulting and business ethics at Vrije Universiteit Amsterdam, where he started in 2001. Since 2023 he also is full professor in consulting at Durham University. Before he has worked as management consultant at KPMG for six years. From 2009 to 2021, he was head of the Management Consulting Research Group at the department Management and Organization, School of Business and Economics at Vrije Universiteit Amsterdam. Here he leads the MSc program on Management Consulting since 2009. In the program he teaches consulting courses on strategy and business ethics. He is also involved in executive education for consultants.

In his research, he combines methods from the humanities with social science methods. In 2010, he published his first monograph with Elgar on *Economic Advice and Rhetoric*. Other studies on management consultants have appeared in the *Journal of Organizational Change Management* (2011), *International Studies of Management & Organization* (2013), *Management Decision* (2015), *Human Relations* (2016), *International Journal of Environmental Research and Public Health* (2018), *German Journal of Human Research Management* (2021, 2022), *and International Journal of Management Reviews* (2022). Themes discussed are consultants' legitimizer roles, their uncertainty management, expert images, stress experiences, leadership at consultancies, work-life conflict, and consultants' intermediary roles between practice and academia. His studies on rhetoric linked to entrepreneurs have been published in *Journal of Business Venturing* (2015), *International Small Business Journal* (2019) and *British Journal of Management* (2022). Studies related to rationality were published in the *Journal of Management Inquiry* (2013) and as monograph with Routledge (2017). A study on moral disengagement has been published in the *Journal of Business Ethics* (2021). Next to scholarly work he publishes in professional journals on these topics.

Chapter 1
Introduction of Jokes-Based Research Methods

1.1 Traditional Studies of Ethical Transgressions in Business

1.1.1 Journalists Reporting on Unethical Business Practices That Include Consultants

From journalists, we learn most about ethical transgressions in business. For long, they are the main informants of scholars in business ethics. What they do report are extreme examples of unethical behaviour, like environmental pollution due to mining, fracking, unsafe oil transport or ecological damage due to bio engineering. Other examples relate to health effects like lung cancer (tobacco industry), DNA damage (nuclear power plants) and lower life expectancy caused by air and water pollution (many industries). On the societal level, reported scandals relate to child labour, new forms of slavery (sweatshops), outsourcing illegal ways of working (mostly by using subcontractors from other countries), gender inequality and various forms of discrimination (everywhere). Journalists also report on money laundering scandals in the financial sector, and about the abundant use of fat, salt, sugar and other additives in the food process industry that encourage overconsumption leading to obesity, indicating companies raise sales at the cost of health. In many service industries, we find pressuring management aiming at increasing profitability, turning burnout into a common job-related illness in a growing number of countries. We learn from journalists it is the most reported job-related illness in the Netherlands for several years now.

Management consultants are partners in crime in many of these scandals. Big 4 (Deloitte, EY, KPMG and PwC) and big 3 (Bain, BCG, McKinsey) consultancies figure prominently in the news on these scandals. They help their clients, for instance, with finding loopholes in the law. Journalists of ICIJ (2014: https://www.icij.org/investigations/luxembourg-leaks/big-4-audit-firms-play-big-role-offshore-murk/) report tax avoidance practices based on the Lux Leaks. Tax advisors of all

© The Author(s) 2023
O. Bouwmeester, *Business Ethics and Critical Consultant Jokes*,
SpringerBriefs in Ethics, https://doi.org/10.1007/978-3-031-10201-1_1

big four consultancies were involved. A second reported practice is overcharging, sometimes resulting in multi-million settlements as with KPMG and BearingPoint (*New York Times*, Apr. 5, 2004: https://www.nytimes.com/2004/04/05/business/kpmg-and-ex-unit-settle-overbilling-case.html). A third example relates to working for corrupt government officials like Isabel dos Santos in Angola (BCG, McKinsey and PwC) or restructuring the South African Revenue Service (SARS) in South Africa under President Zuma, where Bain was complicit in the resulting scandal, and had to settle (*Financial Times*, Oct. 9, 2018: https://www.ft.com/content/f6de62e6-cbb7-11e8-9fe5-24ad351828ab).

Consultants take actively part in the unethical decisions of their clients. The Purdue Pharma case with McKinsey's highest ever settlement is such an example. McKinsey was held responsible for the many overdose deaths (estimated are 450.000 deaths between 1999 and 2018 in the US) of the very addictive OxyContin painkiller, as McKinsey had helped boosting sales of the drug (*BBC News*, Feb. 4, 2021: https://www.bbc.com/news/business-55939224). A related example is the tobacco tactics scandal in Australia, where a Deloitte report commissioned by the tobacco industry was heavily criticized by TobaccoTactics (2020: https://tobaccotactics.org/wiki/deloitte/).

Consultants have also been criticized for giving unfounded or flawed advice to the detriment of their clients, like BCG in the Swedish Karolinska Hospital Scandal, discussed in a blog of Åsa Cajander (2019: https://www.asacajander.se/2019/06/17/kampen-on-karolinska-konsulterna-by-anna-gustafsson-and-lisa-rostlund/). Much discussed is also McKinsey's hunter strategy for Swissair, leading to their collapse, because Swissair started to invest in the wrong airlines (*Economist*, July 19, 2001: https://www.economist.com/business/2001/07/19/a-scary-swiss-meltdown). Next to this, many consultants were involved in insider trading, with journalists reporting several convictions.

Such examples are the top of an iceberg. By studying newspapers, business ethicists learn from journalists about these very extreme cases. The focus is here on what went extremely wrong. Therefore this overview based on what journalists report is not representative for the full spectrum of moral transgressions in the corporate world. What about the more daily forms of unethical behaviour in the business world? How could we study them? Are journalists and their accounts our only sources to study ethical transgressions in business, or do we have more options?

As business ethics is a rather theoretical field dominated by philosophers, the ways to study ethical transgressions in business are limited. In addition, common empirical methods of social scientists have not been developed to study the research questions of business ethicists. That makes business ethics a field of study that is very dependent on non-academic sources. Scholars in business ethics could take more responsibility for developing the methods they need, to study ethics cases in business more accurately, covering individual business behaviours as well as how business life is organized. However, philosophers trained in ethics might feel they are not well prepared for this. Therefore, the current book seeks to answer the question *how business ethics can develop new tailored research methods to study ethical transgressions in professional contexts.*

1.1 Traditional Studies of Ethical Transgressions in Business

I will explore the raised method question by taking criticized consultant practices as a research context for this book. If we can find new ways to let consultants share their experiences, instead of only relying on what journalists report, we might be able to learn a lot more about business ethical transgressions, also in other business fields. Consultants know about their own unethical practices, and they have designed codes of conduct to prevent them. Moreover, management consultants are very knowledgeable as partners in crime. As illustrated above, they are involved in many scandals co-created with their clients.

What makes the ethics question difficult to study, is that confidentiality agreements hinder consultants to share experiences. Opening up might even hurt their clients' and consultants' own reputations. That means, in spite of their rich knowledge, it will be a challenge to motivate consultants to share their insights. Research in business ethics will also be subject to social desirability bias. One journalist reported this very same experience when talking to investment bankers about their unethical behaviours related to the banking crisis (cf. Luyendijk, 2015). Therefore, many journalistic accounts have been based on court cases, on "leaks" documents, and on what whistle-blowers report. It really is a challenge, to study real-life cases of unethical business behaviours.

Social scientists may have encountered unethical business behaviours in their research as well, and they must have faced the same obstacles. Therefore, it is good to first see how past academic studies exploring aspects of consultant ethics did arrive at their results. Before introducing new methods to study ethical transgressions in business, we should know what kind of research has been done in the example case of consultants, as one of the key players in the business field. What methods have been practiced up till now, and what ethical issues have been reported?

1.1.2 Academic Studies on Consultants' Ethics and Their Methods

Some recent reviews and an Oxford Handbook of Management Consulting indicate studies on consultants have increased over the years (Bouwmeester et al., 2022; Cerruti et al., 2019; Kipping & Clark, 2012; Mosonyi et al., 2020). While ethics is addressed in the Oxford Handbook of Management Consulting as an area of interest (Kipping & Clark, 2012; Krehmeyer & Freeman, 2012), the literature on ethics in consulting is still very nascent. Only ten consultant studies could be found with ethics as the main focus. Other studies are touching on the topic, but it is not the key theme studied.

All consultant studies touching on ethics will be reviewed for the critical themes addressed, and the ten key studies also for the research methods used, which are mostly traditional such as interviews, surveys and case studies. Regarding themes, consultant literature pictures clients as the victims of consultants mainly. The issue of consultants and clients as partners in crime that we can learn from journalists is not addressed yet in academic literature on consultants' ethics. This might indicate that used methods are not so well able to pass beyond the barriers of social desirability bias yet, and maybe researcher bias plays a role as well.

The first theme discussed in the literature on consultant ethics relates to expertise. When recommendations have been given with damaging effects on the client, the reason can be consultants' incompetence (e.g. Alvesson & Johansson, 2002; Bouwmeester & Stiekema, 2015; Exton, 1982; Sturdy, 2009). McKenna (2006, p. 142) illustrates, for instance, how incompetence has harmed a client. Consultants working for a non-profit organization assume that non-profits are always inefficiently managed. Such an assumption is clearly based on overgeneralization and indicates a superficial judgement. Likewise, a case study by McKay (2000, p. 295) mentions a group of consultants who did everything wrong in their assignment, and as a consequence, were dismissed. Such examples happen often enough to be noticed. However, clients can be part of the problem when things go wrong. The German philosopher Sloterdijk argues that consultants very well know that their expertise is limited (Sloterdijk, 2006, p. 107). However, such self-knowledge does not always apply to incompetent clients, by him referred to as "Inkompetenzträger". Poulfelt (1997, p. 69) likewise acknowledges consultants' superficiality, but adds like Sloterdijk that clients "can also add (unnecessary) fuel to the fire to protect self-esteem and their own image".

A second criticism points at unethical forms of dishonesty and one-sidedness. While consultants consider honesty, authenticity and reliability very important for a good consultant-client relationship (Block, 2000, p. 37; Shaw, 2020, p. 37), the consultant role often requires more flexibility in this respect than commonly assumed as being ethical. Bluffing seems common practice, and overconfidence part of the job (Angner, 2006; Boussebaa, 2008; Bouwmeester, 2013). In addition, in their role as an advocate—or devil's advocate—consultants may draw on selective truth and one-sided perspectives (Mason, 1969; Saxton, 1995). Jackall (1988, p. 142) mentions a tendency of consultants using euphemistic language and trying to focus on the bright side of difficult situations. In contrast, de Caluwé and Witteveen (2001, p. 11) report that consultants, in trying to arouse certain emotions in clients, may also use exaggeration and distortion techniques to mercilessly address clients' limitations. Apart from this Redekop and Heath (2007, p. 42) argue that consultants can get away with dishonest behaviour quite easily. The authors back this up by quoting consultants who claim that it is highly unlikely they will get caught using fallacious figures or manipulating some numbers in a regression analysis (Redekop & Heath, 2007, p. 45).

The third issue implies dishonesty as well. Overcharging means consultants do not sufficiently live up to the conditions as stated in the contract (Shaw, 2020, p. 33) which makes them unreliable. Redekop and Heath (2007, p. 44) explain as with dishonesty: "It is not that consultants are necessarily greedier than anyone else, it is only that they are in a unique position to capitalize on it". As clients can hardly control the time consultants spend on their assignments, they can write hours they do not work, as long as the client is satisfied with the end result. Kakabadse et al. (2006, p. 458) cite some consultants who feel uncomfortable with this practice, a sentiment

1.1 Traditional Studies of Ethical Transgressions in Business

found in Alvesson and Johansson (2002) as well. Overcharging or double-billing is more common when consultant services are in high demand. Still, Bergh and Gibbons (2011) argue that research does not support the criticism that consultants overcharge systematically and in general. When the demand for consultant services goes down, prices go down as well. Consultants' strong commercial focus is also visible in the practice known as "sell on" which is extending or renewing contracts as long as you can, no matter if it benefits the client. It is an unethical practice discussed by many authors (see O'Mahoney, 2011, pp. 107–108; Jones, 2003, p. 275; Rassam & Oates, 1991, p. 25; Sturdy, 1997, p. 401).

Fourth, when consultants work with clients, they do not always take the whole client system into account. Although serving the client's interest is considered very important (Shaw, 2020, p. 36), interests of the primary client are not necessarily aligned with the interests of all employees, or other relevant external stakeholders (see Bouwmeester & Stiekema, 2015; Poulfelt, 1997; Schein, 1997; Sturdy, 2009). For instance, IT assignments have the potential of increasing efficiency but do not always benefit employees. Sometimes they lose their jobs, in other cases, the work changes. An example is remote working and flex office designs invented by consultants. They can decrease short-term sick leave, but often increase long-term sick leave, feelings of anonymity and concentration problems (Bouwmeester, 2017, pp. 113–121).

Finally, some criticisms relate to internal stakeholder interests at consultancies themselves. Managing partners are not so ethical when relating to client employees, and they seem as commercially focused when it comes to their own employees (Heller, 2002; Krehmeyer & Freeman, 2012; O'Mahoney, 2011; Sturdy, 2009). This criticism aligns with studies reporting high levels of stress and work-life conflict, suggesting that consultants have very demanding managers (Alvesson & Einola, 2018; Bouwmeester & Kok, 2018; Meriläinen et al., 2004; Mühlhaus & Bouwmeester, 2016; Noury et al., 2017). Scholars have also pointed at the metaphor of prostitution (Alvesson & Johansson, 2002, p. 230; Jackall, 1988, p. 143), also suggesting their management is asking too much.

From a methods perspective, some of the criticisms discussed in ten academic articles with a main focus on consultant ethics are inspired by popular press such as newspaper articles, or references to journalistic books (i.e. Ashford, 1998; Micklethwaite & Wooldridge, 1996), autobiographical work (i.e. Pinault, 2000) or other more popular accounts like novels (i.e. Kihn, 2012). Still, more common is to use references to other academic studies, and sometimes own primary data is generated. Table 1.1 gives an overview of the main methods relied on in the ten articles where the focus on consultant ethics is central.

References to other theoretical or empirical work are the dominant source in all ten articles. Studies also use own interview data or survey results. The two studies that refer explicitly to popular press, cite articles from newspapers or magazines and various non-fiction books as illustration of a theoretical argument. Probably we could learn more from these sources. For instance, as indicated before, from the Purdue Pharma case we could learn that McKinsey and their client acted as partners in crime. The TV series House of Lies illustrates similar cases. It is based on a novel inspired by the experiences of Kihn (2012), an ex-consultant at Booz Allan Hamilton.

Table 1.1 Methods used in earlier studies on ethics in management consulting

Sources	Referencing		Interviews	Surveys	Case study
Articles	Other studies	Popular press			
Allen and Davis (1993)	×			×	
Bouwmeester and Kok (2018)	×		×		
Bouwmeester and Stiekema (2015)	×			×	
Krehmeyer and Freeman (2012)	×	×			
McKay (2000)	×		×		×
O'Mahoney (2011)	×		×		
Poulfelt (1997)	×				
Redekop and Heath (2007)	×		×		
Shaw (2020)	×				
Sturdy (2009)	×	×			

Still, this partner-in-crime perspective is missing in academic literature, whereas it seems a credible observation. In addition, Allen and Davis (1993) are left with many unanswered questions after their survey. Redekop and Heath (2007) try to follow up on these questions with an interview study, but their results stay very tentative. Currently, we seem to miss out on some relevant issues. The question is how to better engage in empirical research on all ethical issues and how to invite more honest responses, given the challenges of social desirability bias, moral disengagement or sheer denial. What research methods could help scholars in ethics to generate better results on ethical transgressions and ethical dilemmas in business?

1.2 Unethical Business Practices and Public Jokes

1.2.1 Literature Studies and Ethics

As demonstrated in the context of consulting, academic studies that explore examples of ethical transgressions empirically are comparatively rare. Business ethics has a rather limited tradition in studying ethical transgressions empirically, mainly due to a lack of tailored empirical research methods. The field of ethics is mainly philosophical and prefers to reflect on theoretical cases and thought experiments, next to business cases provided by journalists.

Most empirical work on ethics is done by moral psychologists, often in experimental settings, and by organization theorists in CSR studies. Empirical research in

1.2 Unethical Business Practices and Public Jokes

business ethics remains a challenge, as reflecting in interviews on ethical transgressions experienced in the business context is not easy, and the same applies to giving honest personal answers in a survey. Feelings of shame or fear for lack of control over interpretations by researchers create social desirability bias. Many respondents stay silent when asked about their own unethical business behaviours. They even feel constrained to talk about ethical transgression they have witnessed (cf. Luyendijk, 2015). It is not easy to start a reflection on ethical challenges in business, on behaviour that is far from heroic, or when you failed to face a moral challenge (cf. Hermanowicz, 2002).

While in ethics there is not much of an empirical research tradition, Nussbaum (1995, 2001) could be considered an exception. She has studied novels and tragedies as a way to learn more about ethical traditions in the past and learn how ethical dilemmas were experienced at that time and place. Novels, tragedies or comedies can illustrate how their main characters experience moral struggles that mirror real life. Likewise, we could study novels, comedies or tragedies situated in a current business context, to learn more about current moral challenges. For older professions like lawyers, policemen or professors there have been written such novels and plays that could be used. However, related to the new profession of management consultants there are not so many novels, and novels are not very up to date usually. They span longer time periods in their historical accounts.

Inspired by literature analysis, an alternative source are critical business jokes and cartoons as published on websites, or in newspapers and business magazines. Some studies have hinted at their usefulness for research. For example, Parker (2007, p. 88) suggests that critical representations of popular culture might have the potential to support an ethical agenda. Especially critical cartoons make a moral appeal. Sturdy et al. (2008, p. 142) suggest that there might be a link between humour and ethics, "perhaps". Galanter argues that jokes may "reveal something about our society and ourselves that may otherwise elude us" (Galanter, 2005, p. 19). Therefore, this book seeks to explore how critical business jokes can be part of research methods in the field of business ethics, as there are many critical business jokes on consultants and their ethics.

Similar to tragedy and comedy, jokes and cartoons illustrate what deserves critical attention, including transgressive behaviour of an unethical kind. In the field of consulting such jokes are prominent, next to jokes on lack of work-life balance or an overly strong interest in technological gadgets. Especially the jokes on ethics can be a source for study. Promising is, that jokes are only perceived as funny, if audiences can recognize the ridiculed behaviour. Moreover, jokes play with what is right or wrong, normal or absurd, and timely or outdated. They activate common norms and standards, including ethical ones, by showing norm violation. For that reason, jokes might be able to enrich traditional research methods like interview and survey studies in a way that they become more useful for business ethics research. It is these kinds of methods we want to discuss further. The question is how such jokes-based methods can be used for studying business ethical transgressions.

1.2.2 Humour Theories and Joking About Unethical Practices

Why is it, that jokes or cartoons are used to articulate unethical practices in business? Or to criticize behaviour of politicians? Unethical behaviour has a big share in business jokes, next to illustrations of absurdity, stupidity, ugliness and violations of particular social standards. Indeed, the three most discussed humour theories, incongruity theory, relief theory and superiority theory all indicate the links between humour and moral standards (Watson, 2015).

First, incongruity theory claims that something is funny because it is unexpected, unusual or surprising (Meyer, 2000; Mulder & Nijholt, 2002; Veatch, 1998). The usual serves as the norm, which is unsettled by a surprising punch line. In consultant jokes, the usual can be that consultants are expected to behave as experts and that they can give direction. An incongruity is that they demonstrate an apparent lack of ability. Incongruity theory claims that the surprise creates the fun. The next joke illustrates such an incongruity:

> A client with one consultant knows what to do. A client with two consultants is never sure. (http://www.ronspace.org/consult.htm)

Veatch (1998) criticizes incongruity theory while also building on it. He argues like Bergson (2008, p. 25) that not all incongruities are funny. He adds two necessary conditions that have to be fulfilled simultaneously. First, jokes need to tell something that is emotionally absurd, which implies an offense of what you think is proper, acceptable or just. If an incongruity is only strange, it does not cause enough energy for laughter. However, if the emotional absurdity is too harsh, people can get offended. Veatch's humour theory therefore requires a *mild* offence of the shared moral, social or aesthetic norms and values of an audience, which is the absurdity condition: "the perceiver has in mind a view of the situation as constituting a violation of a "subjective moral principle"" (Veatch, 1998, p. 163). Second condition is that jokes have to characterize a situation that can be seen as normal, something that happens more often, something people can recognize: "the perceiver has in mind a predominating view of the situation as being normal" (Veatch, 1998, p. 164). These two conditions remind of Aristotle's view in the Poetic (1988, p. 1449a), Nichomachean Ethics (1985, p. 1128a) and Rhetoric (1991, p. 1419b), where he argues that real humour should not hurt. Humour has to be entertaining by finding a middle way between being boring and being insulting. It is playing with right and wrong, acceptable and unacceptable, or normal and absurd. That makes humour a perfect vehicle to express moral criticisms mildly, in a way that is not too painful.

Second is the relief theory that adds a psychological dimension to explaining what humour does, which is coping with a difficult situation. While humour can very well serve this purpose, it may serve other purposes as well, which makes it a less general humour theory. The theory also claims that laughter can release the psychic energy that is needed to suppress feelings in taboo areas, like sex or death, and unethical activities belong here too. When taboo thoughts are triggered by humour, the theory

1.2 Unethical Business Practices and Public Jokes

explains that the release of energy results in laughter (Billig, 2005, p. 155; see also Downe, 1999; Meyer, 2000; Mulder & Nijholt, 2002). The relief theory explains coping humour, which is very personal and can also be self-derogative. By doing so, it can liberate feelings of pain, shame or embarrassment as illustrated in the joke:

> Did you hear about the Partner
> … that was so egotistical that even the other Partners noticed?
> (http://www.weitzenegger.de/en/to/jokes.html)

The joke is written in the second person and invites a reading of workplace humour shared between consultants who feel unhappy about their manager's behaviour. When coping jokes criticize such questionable partner behaviour, they enter into a taboo sphere. Consultants are supposed to respect these managing partners, and partners are expected to not only care for themselves. Laughter can help to make such a stressful situation more manageable and less overwhelming. Jokes can also make such partner behaviour more discussable than it would normally be. Coping humour has been studied in other challenging work contexts. Tracy et al. (2006, p. 291) have observed firefighters who "raise their position by laughing at themselves". Coping humour has also been found by Downe (1999), as it appeared in the work life of Costa Rican prostitutes. It is the humour of insiders that work on the edge of what they can handle. One of these edges can be what we consider morally problematic in our professional field. While the mentioned studies observe workplace humour in context, coping humour is also visible in Internet jokes, then illustrating more general patterns like working for selfish partners as in the presented consulting joke, which is not a unique experience. Many consultants will recognize the feeling.

Third is the superiority theory, claiming that people predominantly laugh at the misfortunes of others, and so create insider and outsider groups. Outsiders are put down as not being up to relevant standards in terms of fashion, status, or ethics. Early illustrations of this form of humour can be found in classic philosophy (cf. Aristotle, 1988, p. 1449a), and more pronounced in Hobbes (1991, p. 43). Humiliation of others is seen as an important trigger for laughter (Bergson, 2008, p. 93). Superiority theory assumes that laughter creates a distance between those who laugh, and the subjects of their laughter (Lennox Terrion & Ashforth, 2002). By laughing, the in-group marks certain behaviours or beliefs of outsiders as undesirable or unworthy. Deviant behaviour of outsiders is censored by laughter (Ferguson & Ford, 2008; Meyer, 2000). The next joke illustrates how consultants are made an inferior outsider group:

> Q. Why is a consultant so called?
> A. Because he first cons and then insults you.
> (http://allthingsconsulting.blogspot.com/)

Censoring outsiders involves creating norms and values to support humorous judgments about others' inferior behaviours. Doing so, can help excluding outsiders, and strengthening insider group identities and own value systems (Cooper, 2008; Greatbatch & Clark, 2003; Romero & Pescosolido, 2008; Sturdy et al., 2010). By setting insider norms and excluding those that do not meet these norms, superiority jokes have great potential to express ethical criticism, and to correct behaviour that is seen as socially unacceptable (Bergson, 2008, p. 17).

The three humour theories can all explain how not meeting standards or expectations leads to incongruities of different kinds. The superiority and relief theory add specific psychological motives to the incongruity construction, while Veatch (1998) chooses a more general criterion by speaking of emotional absurdities, with the mild violation of norms as a condition for humour. In addition, the normality condition is quite essential for understanding humour as well. It implies that jokes need to signal something familiar, something we can recognize, even though it might be unexpected, inferior or somewhat taboo.

In an empirical study the condition of mild norm violation as assumed by Veatch (1998) is tested, based on a "benign-violation hypothesis" (McGraw & Warren, 2010, p. 1142). The authors find that benign moral violations indeed generate laughter more often than violations that are not benign, or when norm violation is absent. The study also finds that humour allows for mixed emotions like being both disgusted and amused by the norm violation, in which amusement serves a communicative function: "Laughter and amusement signal to the world that a violation is indeed okay" (McGraw & Warren, 2010, p. 1148).

Figure 1.1 shows how the three forms of humour share that they can signal ethical criticisms. Articulating mild ethical norm violation creates an incongruity. Doing so can be based on different motives: a coping motive in relief theory or a put-down motive in superiority theory, while still meeting the two conditions of emotional absurdity and normality as stated by Veatch (1998).

As superiority humour creates an insider–outsider division, it is in Fig. 1.1 characterized as outsider humour. It can be the humour of clients or their employees about consultants. Coping humour is more self-critical, and here depicted as insider humour. It can be the humour of consultants about consultants. Both forms of humour demand normality and emotional absurdity due to mild norm violation.

By accepting the normality condition as an essential feature of humour, we must also agree that critical business jokes have the ability to address real ethical concerns that people experience in their work life as argued by Galanter (2005). They illustrate norm violations and activate the violated norms at the same time. One may object that jokes do not tell literal truths, as they often exaggerate, distort, stereotype or use irony, which makes it difficult to see through them. Indeed, you cannot take a joke at face value. Jokes need interpretation, just like metaphors (cf. Cornelissen & Kafouros, 2008). Or as Wilk (2021, p. 68) argues, jokes: "kinda-sorta" tell us truths.

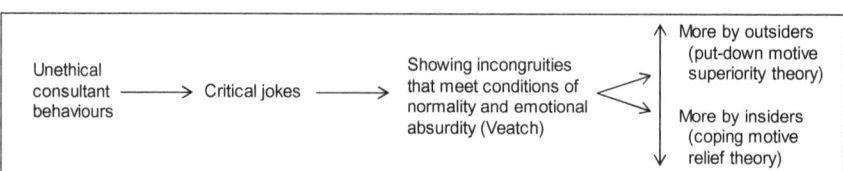

Fig. 1.1 Humour perspectives in jokes stating ethical critique

"The truths they tell, then, are second order." But when we get the joke, "the "aha!" moment of the joke gives us knowledge about ourselves, our communities, and our shared believes."

The meaning of the word joke usually includes text jokes, cartoons, memes, short video jokes and other funny expressions. Sometimes I want to emphasize subcategories, like cartoons, which are visually supported jokes, or text-only jokes, which I will characterize then as *text jokes* in these cases. Usually, I refer to the broader category of jokes in the book.

1.2.3 Jokes-Based Research Methods and Research Ethics

Jokes have the potential of being used in unethical ways. There is humour that discriminates, stereotypes, stigmatizes, or punches down, this way intentionally harming the targets of such jokes (Billig, 2005; De Sousa, 1987; Julin, 2021; Zaldivar, 2021). When using critical jokes as part of research, this could negatively affect jokes-based research methods. For instance, when identifying as a researcher with the critical joke, and thus voicing the ethical criticism to the member of the profession you study, you may become judgemental yourself. It is important to be reflective here. By using jokes, you run a risk that you start stigmatizing or stereotyping yourself, just as when being judgmental in normal language. That is not what should happen when integrating jokes in your research methods. You may be critical towards unethical business behaviours yourself, but the method you use should not be judgemental, stereotyping, discriminating, stigmatizing or leading in any way. That would spoil the results of your research completely.

To keep your own ethical standards high as researcher, it is important to be clear during research and in writing that it is not the researcher that makes the joke with the intent to criticize the practice of the business professional joked about. The jokes presented are anonymous Internet jokes. They need to be presented as such. They have been made by outsiders or insiders or both—the jokes do not tell. They are just used to be interpreted in light of the experiences of the interviewee, or the respondent in a survey. When using the joke for illustration in a theoretical or empirical argument, or in content analysis, the researcher should be careful to let the joke speak for itself. It should be clear where the researchers' interpretations begin, where the joke ends, or where the interviewee or respondent speaks and interprets. Therefore, in the remainder of the book, distinctions between illustrative jokes, interpretations and voice will be made transparent. As reader you are invited to feel how that works.

The positive effect jokes are allowed to have on research participants in interview or survey studies, or on readers interpreting research findings and theoretical explorations, is that they frame unethical practice as a benign or mild norm violation, the ones many of us could laugh about. That may help to reduce social desirability bias, while at the same time the jokes introduce the topic, being the kind of transgression or practice to be discussed. The jokes lighten up the topic. Therefore, the amusement invoked by the humorous form of expression may help to create a play frame, and an emotional state in which moral transgressions can be better shared, discussed and explored (cf. McGraw & Warren, 2010; Sturdy et al., 2008; Veatch, 1998).

1.3 Outline and Contributions

This book aims to develop new research methods in business ethics by making use of the close relationship between critical business jokes and moral critique. First, critical business jokes can enrich our research methods by illustrating what is unethical in consultants' business practices, second, they can be used as prompts for reflection in open interviews, third they can serve as statements to reflect on in rating questions in a survey, and fourth they can be a source for content analysis. While these methods are applied to consultant ethics, all business contexts where critical business jokes abound could fit, such as with unethical bankers, lawyers, the unethical impact of some technological innovations, etc.

When jokes become part of these research methods, the methods undergo a change. In that sense, they become different methods. For instance, when illustrating empirical or theoretical arguments with jokes, the illustration is not a normal mirror image as it commonly is. Instead, the illustration makes fun of ethical norm violation, which activates our values and guides our interpretation. Sampling, selection and the ease of interpretation become key for success, as you better should not have to explain a joke too much. Second, when jokes guide an interview, the selected jokes partly replace the topic list. They introduce the topics. Jokes change the dynamic during the conversation. Giving the interviewee room for interpretation becomes important. How to ask follow-up questions to make connections with related interviewee experiences is important as well, as the jokes are only a first trigger to move to these experiences. Third, when adding jokes to a survey, joke selection deserves careful attention (which topics, visual or text form, etc.), and the formulation of interpretative options (can you sufficiently cover relevant interpretations up front)? Finally, when using jokes as data for content analysis, implications for the method relate to searching (does your strategy yield enough results), how to set boundaries to the sample and how to interpret, as the researcher should be sufficiently able to distinguish fact from fiction. Adding jokes to these four methods makes a methodological difference to all of them.

Chapter 2 discusses the first method of using jokes as illustrations in theoretical or empirical arguments. In order to be useful as illustration in research, it needs to be clear first how well business jokes are able to illustrate relevant ethical transgressions in business. To find out, the strength of the illustration method is demonstrated for a top ten of ethical transgressions in consulting that builds on Bouwmeester (2020). The top ten is based on over 100 interviews. The chapter shows what level of coverage business jokes can provide in illustrating these ethical transgressions that are all in conflict with various parts of the code of conduct for consultants. Benefits of a jokes-as-illustration method are that the method helps to add emphasis,

1.3 Outline and Contributions

urgency and visibility to relevant aspects of well-known business ethical transgressions. With a sample of almost 100 public text jokes on consultants, covering various topics including ethics, the topical coverage was very good. Limitations were that new issues linked to digitalization and privacy were less well covered, as public jokes seem to lag behind a bit. Secondly, the amount of detail provided in text jokes is more limited than what interviews can offer. Jokes emphasize details that illustrate essential aspects of ethical transgressions, leaving out other details that do not help to make the point. The jokes-based illustration method is close to what is common practice in philosophy, where theoretical arguments can be accompanied by fictional illustrations and thought experiments. In addition, the jokes-based illustration method can be relevant to social science researchers, as jokes can add a normative interpretation to illustrated research findings. With these characteristics, the jokes-based illustration method can help with answering descriptive and evaluative research questions. Still, as jokes are no mirror image, interpretations are needed.

Chapter 3 discusses the second method of using jokes as prompts for reflection in open interviews. The jokes-based open interview method helps to answer explorative research questions. The method has been applied to the topic of overly pressuring leadership in consulting (cf. Bouwmeester & Kok, 2018). During the interviews, consultants were invited to reflect on leadership experiences in consulting based on two cartoons and one text joke, illustrating pressuring leadership. After this, they were asked to compare their joke interpretations with their own experiences and to elaborate on these. The jokes give structure to the interview like a topic list, but invite more association, elaboration and qualification of statements in the jokes. Jokes require interpretation much like metaphors, suggesting some elements might be different or less extreme in reality. As jokes show themselves as being jokes, people know very well how to relate to the genre. Benefits of the method are that rapport improves, that interviewees get more talkative, and that they get better access to their relevant memories, thus better crossing the boundaries of social desirability bias and taboo as compared to traditional interview methods. A method limitation is that jokes could be seen as leading by reviewers, because jokes also activate judgements of what we should see as normal or absurd from a moral point of view. This makes it key to clearly describe how the jokes have been used, where the responses of the interviewees start and where the influence of the jokes end. The chapter concludes with some reviewer concerns, and possible responses.

Chapter 4 presents a jokes-based survey method. This third method uses cartoons and their statements as material to be rated, next to traditional rating questions on the same topic. The jokes-based survey method helps to answer descriptive research questions. This type of mixed method has been applied to the critique that consultants lack expertise (cf. Bouwmeester & Stiekema, 2015). Stakeholder opinions on consultants' expertise are compared, including clients, client employees, consultants, academics and outsiders. Triangulation of the results gives similar results when it comes to stakeholder opinions, with client employees as the most critical stakeholder, apparently suffering the most from consultants' perceived lack of expertise. Benefits of the method compared to traditional survey methods are that it offers a new kind of control question, it helps to increase response and completion rates and triggers memories differently with humour and visualizations. These benefits work especially when reflecting on ethical issues, where people might be reluctant to open up. The chapter concludes with possible reviewer concerns and responses.

Chapter 5 explores the possibilities of content analysis of jokes as the fourth method as applied in Bouwmeester (2013) on the topic of uncertainties in the consultant-client relation. Jokes-based content analysis helps to answer explorative research questions. Text jokes and cartoons have been sampled related to the topic, analysing how both sides relate to the uncertainties. The method not only replicates several insights from the literature on consultants but also adds more detail on topics like bluffing, and on client uses of consultant uncertainties. Validity of the method is very dependent on the sample size, as more jokes allow for more data triangulation, which can help to sort out facts from fiction. Benefits of using jokes for content analysis are the accessibility of this new data source, and the new insights it can offer on business ethical questions. The chapter concludes with discussing how to relate to possible reviewer concerns.

Chapter 6 starts with a comparative discussion of each of the four methods, their strengths, and validity issues that relate to the use of jokes in the various methods. The chapter concludes with a philosophical reflection on the question of why jokes are such a helpful genre when studying business ethical transgressions, which relates to both the normative and positive qualities of jokes. The book contributes to the development of new empirical research methods suitable to the field of business ethics, where social desirability bias, taboo and shame experiences are serious obstacles to the effective use of more common empirical research methods. The methods also fit other areas of norm transgression, such as those related to traditions, fashions, cultures, art, technology, etc., thus aiming at scholars and researchers in business ethics, corporate social responsibility, and the social sciences more broadly. As a secondary contribution the book adds to the consultant literature by mapping the more common ethical transgressions in this field. Especially in Chap. 2 consultants, future consultants and their clients may learn about the various ethical issues they could encounter when working together.

References

Allen, J., & Davis, D. (1993). Assessing some determinant effects of ethical consulting behavior: The case of personal and professional values. *Journal of Business Ethics, 12*(6), 449–458.
Alvesson, M., & Einola, K. (2018). Excessive work regimes and functional stupidity. *German Journal of Human Resource Management, 32*(3–4), 283–296.
Alvesson, M., & Johansson, A. (2002). Professionalism and politics in management consultancy work. In T. Clark & R. Fincham (Eds.), *Critical consulting: New perspectives on the management advice industry* (pp. 228–246). Wiley-Blackwell.
Angner, E. (2006). Economists as experts: Overconfidence in theory and practice. *Journal of Economic Methodology, 13*(1), 1–24.
Aristoteles, O. (1985). *Nikomachische Ethik*. Meiner Verlag.
Aristoteles, O. (1988). *Poëtica*. Athenaeum-Polak & Van Gennep.

References

Aristotle, O., & Kennedy, G. A. (1991). *On rhetoric: A theory of civic discourse*. Oxford University Press.

Ashford, M. (1998). *Con tricks: The shadowy world of management consultancy and how to make it work for you*. Simon & Schuster.

Bergh, D. D., & Gibbons, P. (2011). The stock market reaction to the hiring of management consultants: A signalling theory approach. *Journal of Management Studies*.

Bergson, H. (2008). *Laughter: An essay on the meaning of the comic*. Arc Manor.

Billig, M. (2005). *Laughter and ridicule: Towards a social critique of humour*. Sage.

Block, P. (2000). *Flawless consulting: A guide to getting your expertise used*. Jossey-Bass/Pfeiffer.

Boussebaa, M. (2008). Book Review: Are Consultants Simply Bluffing? Sociologie du conseil en management by Michel Villette. *Organization, 15*(2), 298-300.

Bouwmeester, O. (2013). Consultant jokes about managing uncertainty: Coping through humor. *International Studies of Management & Organization, 43*(3), 41–57.

Bouwmeester, O. (2017). *The social construction of rationality: Policy debates and the power of good reasons*. Routledge.

Bouwmeester, O. (2020). Consultants en ethiek: Een top tien van pijnpunten. *M&C Quarterly, 2020*(2), 44–49.

Bouwmeester, O., Heusinkveld, S., & Tjemkes, B. (2022). Intermediaries in the relevance-gap debate: A systematic review of consulting roles. *International Journal of Management Reviews, 24*(1), 51-77 .

Bouwmeester, O., & Kok, T. E. (2018). Moral or dirty leadership: A qualitative study on how juniors are managed in Dutch consultancies. *International Journal of Environmental Research and Public Health, 15*(11), 2506.

Bouwmeester, O., & Stiekema, J. (2015). The paradoxical image of consultant expertise: A rhetorical deconstruction. *Management Decision, 53*(10), 2433–2456.

Caluwe de, L. I. A., & Witteveen, A. (2001). Organisatieadvies: Wat is dat? In L. I. A. de Caluwe & A. Witteveen (Eds.), *Organisatieadvies: Wat is dat?* (pp. 9–17). Scriptum.

Cerruti, C., Tavoletti, E., & Grieco, C. (2019). Management consulting: A review of fifty years of scholarly research. *Management Research Review, 42*(8), 902–925.

Cooper, C. (2008). Elucidating the bonds of workplace humor: A relational process model. *Human Relations, 61*(8), 1087–1115.

Cornelissen, J. P., & Kafouros, M. (2008). Metaphors and theory building in organization theory: What determines the impact of a metaphor on theory? *British Journal of Management, 19*(4), 365–379.

De Sousa, R. (1987). *The rationality of emotion*. Mit Press.

Downe, P. J. (1999). Laughing when it hurts: Humor and violence in the lives of costa rican prostitutes. *Women's Studies International Forum, 22*(1), 63–78.

Exton, W. (1982). Ethical and moral considerations and the principle of excellence in management consulting. *Journal of Business Ethics, 1*(3), 211–218.

Ferguson, M. A., & Ford, T. E. (2008). Disparagement humor: A theoretical and empirical review of psychoanalytic, superiority, and social identity theories. *Humor-International Journal of Humor Research, 21*(3), 283–312.

Galanter, M. (2005). *Lowering the bar: Lawyer jokes and legal culture*. University of Wisconsin Press.

Greatbatch, D., & Clark, T. (2003). Displaying group cohesiveness: Humour and laughter in the public lectures of management gurus. *Human Relations, 56*(12), 1515.

Heller, F. (2002). What next? More critique of consultants, gurus and managers. In T. Clark & R. Fincham (Eds.), *Critical consulting: New perspectives on the management advice industry* (pp. 260–272). Blackwell.

Hermanowicz, J. C. (2002). The great interview: 25 strategies for studying people in bed. *Qualitative sociology, 25*(4), 479–499. https://doi.org/10.1023/A:1021062932081.

Hobbes, T. (1991). *Leviathan*. Cambridge University Press.

Jackall, R. (1988). *Moral mazes* (Vol. 4). Oxford University Press.

Jones, M. (2003). The expert system: Constructing expertise in an IT/management consultancy. *Information and Organization, 13*(4), 257–284.

Julin, G. (2021). What's the punch line?: Punching up and down in the comic thunderdome. In J. M. Henrigillis & S. Gimbel (Eds.), *It's funny'cause it's true: The Lighthearted Philosophers' Society's introduction to philosophy through humor* (pp. 143–155). Lighthearted Philosophers' Society. https://cupola.gettysburg.edu/oer/10/

Kakabadse, N. K., Louchart, E., & Kakabadse, A. (2006). Consultant's role: A qualitative inquiry from the consultant's perspective. *Journal of Management Development, 25*(5), 416–500.

Kihn, M. (2012). *House of lies: How management consultants steel your watch and then tell you the time.* Business Plus.

Kipping, M., & Clark, T. (2012). *The Oxford handbook of management consulting.* OUP Oxford.

Krehmeyer, D., & Freeman, R. E. (2012). Consulting and ethics. *The Oxford handbook of management consulting* (pp. 487–498). Oxford University Press.

Lennox Terrion, J., & Ashforth, B. E. (2002). From "I" to "We": The role of putdown humor and identity in the development of a temporary group. *Human Relations, 55*(1), 55–88.

Luyendijk, J. (2015). *Swimming with sharks: My journey into the world of the bankers* (Vol. 4). Guardian Faber Publishing.

Mason, R. O. (1969). A dialectical approach to strategic planning. *Management Science, 15*(8), B-403–B-414.

McGraw, A. P., & Warren, C. (2010). Benign violations: Making immoral behavior funny. *Psychological Science, 21*(8), 1141–1149.

McKay, R. B. (2000). Consequential utilitarianism: Addressing ethical deficiencies in the municipal landfill siting process. *Journal of Business Ethics, 26*(4), 289–306.

McKenna, C. D. (2006). *The world's newest profession: Management consulting in the twentieth century.* Cambridge University Press.

Meriläinen, S., Tienari, J., Thomas, R., & Davies, A. (2004). Management consultant talk: A cross-cultural comparison of normalizing discourse and resistance. *Organization, 11*(4), 539–564.

Meyer, J. C. (2000). Humor as a double edged sword: Four functions of humor in communication. *Communication Theory, 10*(3), 310–331.

Micklethwaite, J., & Wooldridge, A. (1996). *The witch doctors: making sense of the management gurus.* Times Books.

Mosonyi, S., Empson, L., & Gond, J. P. (2020). Management consulting: Towards an integrative framework of knowledge, identity, and power. *International Journal of Management Reviews, 22*(2), 120–149.

Mühlhaus, J., & Bouwmeester, O. (2016). The paradoxical effect of self-categorization on work stress in a high-status occupation: Insights from management consulting. *Human Relations, 69*(9), 1823–1852.

Mulder, M. P., & Nijholt, A. (2002). *Humour research: State of the art.* University Twente.

Noury, L., Gand, S., & Sardas, J.-C. (2017). Tackling the work-life balance challenge in professional service firms: The impact of projects, organizing, and service characteristics. *Journal of Professions and Organization, 4*(2), 149–178.

Nussbaum, M. (1995). *Poetic justice: The literary imagination and public life.* Beacon Press.

Nussbaum, M. C. (2001). *The fragility of goodness: Luck and ethics in Greek tragedy and philosophy.* Cambridge University Press.

O'Mahoney, J. (2011). Advisory anxieties: Ethical individualisation in the UK consulting industry. *Journal of Business Ethics, 104*(1), 101–113.

Parker, M. (2007). The little book of management bollocks and the culture of organization. In R. Westwood & C. Rhodes (Eds.), *Humour work and organization* (pp. 77–92). Routledge.

Pinault, L. (2000). *Consulting demons: Inside the unscrupulous world of global corporate consulting.* Wiley.

Poulfelt, F. (1997). Ethics for management consultants. *Business Ethics: A European Review, 6*(2), 65–70.

Rassam, C., & Oates, D. (1991). *Management consultancy: The inside story.* Mercury.

Redekop, B. W., & Heath, B. L. (2007). A brief examination of the nature, contexts, and causes of unethical consultant behaviors. *Journal of Practical Consulting, 1*(2), 40–50.

Romero, E., & Pescosolido, A. (2008). Humor and group effectiveness. *Human Relations, 61*(3), 395–418.

Saxton, T. (1995). The impact of third parties on strategic decision making: Roles, timing and organizational outcomes. *Journal of Organizational Change Management, 8*(3), 47–62.

Schein, E. H. (1997). The concept of "client" from a process consultation perspective: A guide for change agents. *Journal of Organizational Change Management*.

Shaw, D. (2020). Aristotle and the management consultants: Shooting for ethical practice. *Philosophy of Management, 19*(1), 21–44.

Sloterdijk, P. (2006). *Im Weltinnenraum des Kapitals. Für eine philosophische Theorie des Globalisierung*. Suhrkamp Verlag.

Sturdy, A. (1997). The consultancy process: An insecure business? *Journal of Management Studies, 34*(3), 389–413.

Sturdy, A. (2009). Popular critiques of consultancy and a politics of management learning? *Management Learning, 40*(4), 457.

Sturdy, A., Clark, T., Fincham, R., & Handley, K. (2008). Management consultancy and humor in action and context. In S. Fineman (Ed.), *The emotional organization: Passions and power* (pp. 134–150). Blackwell.

Sturdy, A., Handley, K., Clark, T., & Fincham, R. (2010). *Management consultancy: Boundaries and knowledge in action*. Oxford University Press.

Tracy, S. J., Myers, K. K., & Scott, C. W. (2006). Cracking jokes and crafting selves: Sensemaking and identity management among human service workers. *Communication Monographs, 73*(3), 283–308.

Veatch, T. C. (1998). A theory of humor. *Humor-International Journal of Humor Research, 11*(2), 161–216.

Watson, C. (2015). A sociologist walks into a bar (and other academic challenges): Towards a methodology of humour. *Sociology, 49*(3), 407–421.

Wilk, T. (2021). Joking as truth-telling. In J. M. Henrigillis & S. Gimbel (Eds.), *It's funny'cause it's true: The Lighthearted Philosophers' Society's Introduction to philosophy through humor* (pp. 63–68). Lighthearted Philosophers' Society. https://cupola.gettysburg.edu/oer/10/

Zaldivar, E. (2021). Tendentious jokes are immoral. In J. M. Henrigillis & S. Gimbel (Eds.), *It's funny'cause it's true: The Lighthearted Philosophers' Society's introduction to philosophy through humor* (pp. 128–134). Lighthearted Philosophers' Society. https://cupola.gettysburg.edu/oer/10/

Used Journalistic Sources

(Accessed June 5, 2021)

Åsa Cajander. (June 17, 2019). https://www.asacajander.se/2019/06/17/kampen-on-karolinska-konsulterna-by-anna-gustafsson-and-lisa-rostlund/.

BBC News. (Feb. 4, 2021). https://www.bbc.com/news/business-55939224.

Economist. (July 19, 2001). https://www.economist.com/business/2001/07/19/a-scary-swiss-meltdown.

Financial Times. (Oct. 9, 2018). https://www.ft.com/content/f6de62e6-cbb7-11e8-9fe5-24ad351828ab.

ICIJ. (2014). https://www.icij.org/investigations/luxembourg-leaks/big-4-audit-firms-play-big-role-offshore-murk/.

New York Times. (Apr. 5, 2004). https://www.nytimes.com/2004/04/05/business/kpmg-and-ex-unit-settle-overbilling-case.html.

TobaccoTactics. (June 16, 2020). https://tobaccotactics.org/wiki/deloitte/.

Internet Sources for Further Reading on Controversies Big 3

(Accessed June 5, 2021)
Bain
https://www.consultancy.co.za/news/1858/athol-williams-leaves-bain-just-six-months-after-joining.
https://en.wikipedia.org/wiki/Bain_%26_Company#South_African_Revenue_Service_Inquiry.

BCG
https://www.icij.org/investigations/luanda-leaks/banking-documents-reveal-consulting-giants-cash-windfall-under-angolan-billionaire-isabel-dos-santos/.
https://globalanticorruptionblog.com/tag/bcg/.
https://en.wikipedia.org/wiki/Boston_Consulting_Group#Controversy.

McKinsey
https://www.trtworld.com/magazine/the-many-times-mckinsey-has-been-embroiled-in-scandals-43996.
https://www.propublica.org/series/mckinseys-rules.
https://en.wikipedia.org/wiki/McKinsey_%26_Company#Controversies.

Internet Sources for Further Reading on Controversies Big 4

(Accessed June 5, 2021)
Deloitte
https://www.justice.gov/opa/pr/deloitte-consulting-llp-agrees-pay-11-million-alleged-false-claims-related-general-services.
https://www.biznews.com/briefs/2020/03/21/deloitte-r150m-settlement-eskom.
https://www.bloomberg.com/news/articles/2019-10-21/deloitte-dragged-into-south-african-state-corruption-scandals.
https://www.bat.com/group/sites/UK__9D9KCY.nsf/vwPagesWebLive/DO8GHFEN.
https://www.afr.com/companies/professional-services/deloitte-looks-to-knock-out-bulk-of-age-discrimination-case-20200921-p55xqx.
https://www.afr.com/companies/professional-services/older-partner-claims-deloitte-forced-him-out-20200805-p55itt.
https://en.wikipedia.org/wiki/Deloitte#Controversies.

EY
https://www.accountingtoday.com/news/e-amp-y-cap-gemini-settle-travel-billing-lawsuit-for-20m.
https://en.wikipedia.org/wiki/Ernst_%26_Young#Public_disputes.

KPMG
https://news.bloombergtax.com/financial-accounting/deloitte-kpmg-pwc-units-fined-in-spain-consulting-cartels.
https://www.cbc.ca/news/business/cra-kmpg-settlement-taxes-1.5154610.
https://www.irishtimes.com/business/kpmg-admits-to-fraud-schemes-in-us-1.486046.
https://www.ft.com/content/973dd064-1802-11da-a14b-0000e0e2511c8.
https://www.dutchnews.nl/news/2017/07/public-prosecutor-settles-kpmg-office-tax-evasion-case/.
https://en.wikipedia.org/wiki/KPMG#Controversies.

References

PwC
https://www.fedortax.com/blog/consulting-company-accenture-pays-200-million-to-settle-tax-claims.
https://en.wikipedia.org/wiki/PricewaterhouseCoopers#Controversies.

Open Access This chapter is licensed under the terms of the Creative Commons Attribution 4.0 International License (http://creativecommons.org/licenses/by/4.0/), which permits use, sharing, adaptation, distribution and reproduction in any medium or format, as long as you give appropriate credit to the original author(s) and the source, provide a link to the Creative Commons license and indicate if changes were made.

The images or other third party material in this chapter are included in the chapter's Creative Commons license, unless indicated otherwise in a credit line to the material. If material is not included in the chapter's Creative Commons license and your intended use is not permitted by statutory regulation or exceeds the permitted use, you will need to obtain permission directly from the copyright holder.

Chapter 2
Jokes That Illustrate Unethical Business Behaviour

2.1 Introduction to a Jokes-Based Method of Illustration

We learn from journalists about extreme unethical behaviours in business. Newspapers report on big settlements, large scandals and environmental disasters. Apart from that, business ethicists do not have so many sources to learn from. Maybe we have some own experiences, or we learn from friends and relatives. Social scientists may do research that touches on business ethics, but journalists report the most. In contrast, the business world itself tries to hide their unethical practices and aims to protect their reputation. This raises the question of how to study ethical transgressions in business, and what are sources for ethics scholars to illustrate what happens, next to what journalists can report.

Social scientists are familiar with method reflections when it comes to empirical research methods. They may be aware of the sampling issues related to the selection of an illustrative case. For philosophers, such reflection is rare, as their methods are assumed to be theoretical. They connect ideas, criticize assumptions or develop and apply principles. Illustration can then be part of a deductive argument, for instance, when Thomson (1985) uses various trolley cases based on the ideas of Philippa Foot, to illustrate situations where deontological ethics better captures our moral intuitions than consequentialist reasoning. In a similar somewhat naïve way, ethicists use business ethics cases based on journalistic accounts. However, this use is not unproblematic, as journalists focus on newsworthiness, for instance, and on extremes. These illustrations might miss more than they may cover. Therefore, also for ethics scholars, it is important to reflect on the limitations of the sources they use for illustration, and how they select their empirical sources. Therefore, empirical illustration needs to be treated like a research method in business ethics.

Underexplored as source for illustration in business ethics are business jokes. They are made and shared in the business context, and they criticize unethical business practices from the inside. They illustrate norm violation, but also activate norms by stressing its funniness and oddity. Critical business jokes draw on insider knowledge and experiences of affected stakeholders. However, how well such jokes can illustrate ethical issues and how well they cover the full spectrum of unethical business practices, we do not know yet. Therefore, we need to find out *how well business jokes can illustrate the relevant ethical issues in a business context*. To answer this question, this chapter presents and evaluates a jokes-based illustration method to show ethical transgressions applied to the context of consultants and their clients. Related method questions are how to search, sample, select and interpret business jokes that serve as an illustration of ethical transgressions.

In the next sections, key values in consultants' codes of conduct will be reviewed first, to set a standard for business behaviours that cross the line of ethics in this field. Second, ten common ethical transgressions will be discussed as shared by consultants. For each of them some publicly available illustrative consultant jokes will be searched, selected and interpreted. They can illustrate all these common business ethical transgressions, in ways relevant both for descriptive and evaluative research. After this, concerns will be discussed related to the possibilities and limitations of the jokes-based illustration method for business ethics, given that jokes are no literal illustrations. As business jokes illustrate the more common, everyday transgressions, they are a new source for illustration in business ethics, complementary to newspaper articles.

2.2 The Issue—Code Violations as Food for Jokes

The new jokes-based method of illustration will be applied to various examples of violating standards of the code of conduct for consultants as reported in the Netherlands. These codes help to set the standards and to prevent ethical transgressions. The reported ethical transgressions are part of the daily work-life of consultants, and the same transgressions are also criticized in business jokes.

In the Netherlands, the code of the OOA (Orde van Organisatiekundigen en Adviseurs) is for individual consultants. The discussed version is from 2014, but it is currently under revision. The Dutch ROA (Raad van Organisatie Adviesbureaus) had the same code, but changed it in 2021. The key values are still the same.

At the moment of writing, there are ca. 200.000 consultants in the Netherlands, half of them independent, half of them employed (CBS, 2021; I&O Research, 2019). Only ca. 2% of them is member of the OOA or ROA (Consultancy.nl, 2015). That seems little, but international consultancies in the Netherlands usually have their own codes of conduct, which makes the number of consultants that commit to a code of conduct somewhat higher.

In the European context, more broadly, many national consultancy associations are members of FEACO and follow the FEACO code. In contrast, OOA and ROA have their own, more extensive code. Consultancies in the US can be members of IMC, also with its own code of conduct. These international codes of consultancies or consultancy associations are all quite similar and intend to articulate the most important ethical norms and values that should be guiding consultants in their work.

2.2 The Issue—Code Violations as Food for Jokes

Table 2.1 Key values addressed in consultancies' codes of conduct

OOA key code	FEACO Code of ethic	IMC USA
Expert	Qualification Quality	Requisite experience, competence knowledge and expertise of assigned staff
Reliable	Clarity contract/finances Confidentiality	Contract clarity Confidentiality
Meticulous	Ethics Transparency	Realistic expectations Integrity
Professionally independent		Independence, objectivity
		Fiscal integrity
		Commitment to the public and the profession

Sources
OOA https://www.ooa.nl/download/?id=17939577 (last accessed: Nov. 2021)
ROA https://www.roa-advies.nl/files/25/ROA%20Gedragscode.pdf (last accessed: Nov. 2021)
FEACO http://www.feaco.org/aboutfeaco/codeofethic (last accessed: Dec. 2020)
ICM https://cdn.ymaws.com/www.imcusa.org/resource/collection/FF4D824A-2E4D-4199-9263-63C5FD63D135/imc_usa_code_of_ethics__final_.pdf (last accessed: Dec. 2020)

They aim to prevent forms of misconduct as criticized by clients, colleagues, and journalists. Still, much unethical behaviour happens under the radar and becomes food for critical business jokes.

Key values in consulting are being qualified for the job (expertise) being transparent regarding contracts (reliability) and putting the client's interests first (meticulousness). Professional independence is mentioned as well, except by FEACO. If consultancies are members of an association such as ROA in the Netherlands, MCA in the UK or the Institute of Management Consultants (IMC) in the US, codes are binding for them, and the same applies to individual consultants that are members of an association. Table 2.1 summarizes what kind of norms and values are stressed in such codes as being key values.

In the past, codes of conduct have been criticized for having little impact, (e.g. Allen & Davis, 1993; Kaptein & Schwartz, 2008; Kubr, 2002; O'Mahoney and Markham, 2013; Webley & Werner, 2008). O'Mahoney (2011) argues they are vague and they shift responsibility from the organization to individual consultants, referring to the experiences of UK consultants. Still, codes help to address what is unethical behaviour in a business context by setting a standard. Criticisms in newspapers or in business jokes are usually at odds with such standards.

From an ethics perspective, codes of conduct can be related to deontology as ethical perspective (Krehmeyer & Freeman, 2012). Deontological ethics tries to define universal principles that can guide our behaviour. This is exactly what a code of conduct tries to do. Poulfelt (1997) considers consequentialism a more helpful ethical perspective for consultants than deontology, as it is difficult for consultants to formulate rules that hold in every situation, because stakeholder interests can be very different or even conflicting. Consequentialists would ask what the consequences are of our behaviour, considering all involved stakeholders. They ask who is harmed, or who will benefit from what consultants recommend to their client. A third perspective is called virtue ethics. It helps asking what kind of person I will become if I behave in certain ways, and how it affects my character. Virtues can be modesty, honesty, courage, etc., and according to Aristoteles (1985), they require moderation: too much courage becomes recklessness, and too much honesty can be perceived as tactless. Shaw (2020) has argued that virtue ethics is the most relevant perspective for consultants, as it is a professional service that very much depends on professional character. We might thus conclude that all three perspectives are relevant and helpful in practice.

Irrespective of a preferred ethical perspective, when it comes to humour all ways of crossing the line can be inspirational for crafting critical business jokes. Lack of virtue or clumsiness can be funny, as can be the less favourite consequences someone suffers (as with a clown). When consultants or stakeholders start making jokes about consultants' unethical behaviours, they illustrate how norms like those stressed in the codes of conduct are mildly violated. This triggers emotional responses that cause laughter among those who know the sector well enough to recognize the normality of the transgression implied in such jokes (Veatch, 1998). As argued earlier, the normality condition of humour explains why popular jokes may give good illustrations, the required mild norm violation why jokes can illustrate unethical behaviour.

2.3 Application—Ten Business Ethical Transgressions Illustrated

2.3.1 *Illustration Method: How to Search and Select Jokes Illustrating the Top Ten*

Recently, ten common business ethical transgressions of consultants have been reported in *M&C Quarterly* a Dutch professional journal for consultants (Bouwmeester, 2020). In this section, these ten transgressions will be illustrated by business jokes, and the question is how well they illustrate and what exactly they could illustrate. As a method, an illustration of ethical transgressions will be applied and evaluated. Jokes are no literal illustration, no mirror image and they emphasize norm violation for those who can understand. Like with metaphors, interpretation is key. As a reader, you are invited to evaluate the interpretations, given the context. Context is given first, illustrations follow; the proof is in the pudding.

To assess how well jokes can illustrate moral transgression, it would be enough to read the top five and their illustrations. The reason for reporting the entire top ten is to show what happens if transgressions become less common. Then there are less jokes to choose from, and illustrative coverage can become less strong, whereas the issues

2.3 Application—Ten Business Ethical Transgressions Illustrated

can still be quite serious. Discussing the full top ten enables a better assessment of the limits of the jokes-based illustration method. I leave it up to the reader to decide how relevant it is to study the illustration method in so much detail, or to skip the reading of transgressions from six to ten.

2.3.2 Illustration Results: A Top Ten Ethical Transgressions in Business Jokes

The top ten in Bouwmeester (2020) was based on 75 interviews with consultants, done between 2017 and 2020. For this book, 51 more interviews from 2021 could be added. Interviews were performed by students of my ethics course in the MSc Management Consulting at Vrije Universiteit Amsterdam. Students have explored ethical challenges experienced by consultants during their consulting career. Most interviews were done face to face, but due to COVID-19, the 2021 interviews were mostly done by video calling. Most interviewed consultants were Dutch, some had a non-Dutch background, and then mostly European. The average age of the interviewed consultants is around 30 years, similar to the average age in big 4 consultancies. That means, the perspective of junior consultants is well represented. Consultants have been asked for their consent and all interviews have been transcribed.

The 51 new interviews support the earlier top ten, but have changed the ranking somewhat, as based on how often the transgressions were reported. Overbilling has entered the top three, due to the new interviews. In total, 112 interviews could be used for identifying the more recurrent ethical challenges mentioned. These issues that made it to the top ten have been mentioned at least 6 times and up to 22 times. Table 2.2 gives an overview of this top ten, what key values from the code of conduct are violated and how many consultants reported the issue.

Table 2.2 Overview of ethical transgressions top ten

Type of ethical transgression:	Violated values from the code of conduct	Times reported
1. Harming interests of client employees	Meticulousness	22
2. Independence under pressure	Professional independence	15
3. Overbilling and selling juniors as seniors	Reliability	15
4. Fake it till you make it	Expertise	12
5. Extending unnecessary work: a revenue model	Meticulousness	11
6. Confidentiality and double billing	Reliability	9
7. Supporting morally dirty clients	Meticulousness	8
8. Underperformance	Expertise	8
9. Insufficient protection of client data	Reliability	6
10. Bending conclusions	Professional independence	6

The jokes-based illustration method introduced here will be used to illustrate this top ten. Illustrative jokes were selected from a compendium of ca. 100 text jokes on consultants that I have collected together with students, and initiated by Oscar Haffmans. Most of these jokes have been found on the Internet, and cover topics like ethics, work-life balance, use of technology, etc. Keywords that Oscar used in his search to create the initial sample were "consultant", "consulting", "consultancy", "management consultant", "management consulting" and "management consultancy". Each of these words was combined with the word "joke", and each search was conducted twice, once with and once without quotation marks. Over the years, more jokes were found and added in a less systematic way. All links to the jokes were last accessed on August 8, 2021. If links would expire, jokes can usually be found somewhere else by searching in google with one line of the joke.

To select jokes from the sample, the joke with the best illustrative value has been chosen. This requires an understanding of the joke, as well as of the ethical issue, that is illustrated. Sometimes only some lines from a list joke were selected, as most other lines were not relevant. Selection criteria have been topical fit (descriptive) and aligned critical message (normative). Below issues from the top ten based on the interviews will be described first, and then illustrated with jokes.

1. **Harming the Interests of Client Employees**

    Interviewees have mentioned mostly the risk of harming employees in client organizations with their work. Particularly challenging are clients who ask consultants for an opinion on individual employees when this is not part of the assignment. Reactions from consultants range from asking to formally extend the scope of the assignment, to sticking to the original assignment. A middle ground is to make clear in very general terms where problems in a department originate so that clients can draw their own conclusions. Consultants do not want to assess employees behind their back, also when they clearly see how an employee or manager is not functioning well. A solution to the problem has once been to offer a training to an entire management team and not just the problematic manager. Still, sometimes consultants give in to such unethical requests of clients, at the cost of employees.

    A similar dilemma occurs when organizational and other stakeholder interests do not tie in well with each other. Examples are automation and rationalization projects. Often well-functioning employees have to leave, while machines or IT systems take over. It is a problem of all times for consultants, but it is never fun, and it requires careful balancing of various stakeholder interests. The issue is that not every innovation is necessary or beneficial from the point of view of the wider client system, although consultants can make money with it. And indeed, they do.

    Illustrative jokes In the sample, many jokes are criticizing the consultant role related to employee interests. Below three examples are selected, the first two showing employee anger indicating their interests have been harmed. The

2.3 Application—Ten Business Ethical Transgressions Illustrated

third is ridiculing the rationalization routine as a one size fits all approach, suggesting many employees will lose their jobs without a real need.

> Did you hear that the post office just recalled their latest stamps? They had pictures of consultants on them…………..and people couldn't work out which side to spit on.
> (www.infolanka.com/jokes/messages/1581.html)
>
> Why are consultants like nuclear weapons?
> If one side has one, the other side has to get one. Once launched, they cannot be recalled. When they land, they screw up everything forever.
> (www.infolanka.com/jokes/messages/1581.html)
>
> There was a glass of water on the table...
> One man says, "It's half full". He is an optimist.
> Second man says, "It's half empty". He is a pessimist.
> Third man says, "It's twice too big". He is a management consultant.
> (http://nowthatisfunny.blogspot.com/2005/10/jokes-about-consultants.html)

Interpretation The first two jokes are targeting consultants, and it is not difficult to imagine how employees feel being a victim of what consultants have done to them. Employees could share such jokes among each other to express their discontent. And maybe consultants share such jokes as well, when they feel somewhat guilty for not taking employee interests into account sufficiently. It is all against the principle of meticulousness (OOA code of conduct), ethics (FEACO code) or integrity (IMC USA code). Meticulousness is also under pressure in the third joke on rationalization, indicating organizations are always too big. The efficiency focus is what consultants are famous for. They downsize organizations, replace people by IT systems and suggest outsourcing strategies. As a result, people lose their jobs and they hold consultants accountable. A consequentialist perspective can best help to indicate how the overall effect of such projects might be considered unethical by harming employee, or other stakeholder interests, especially in cases without an urgent organizational need for the change. The jokes read as outsider jokes, that is, being made by client employees about consultants. The illustrative value of the selected jokes is high. The normality condition of humour explains why there are many more examples to choose from in this category.

2. **Independence Under Pressure**
A feeling of being manipulated when writing down conclusions is number two in the top ten, based on how many consultants mention the issue in the interviews. There are two ways how this happens. The first is that clients want to hear a certain outcome for which the grounds are insufficient. In the examples mentioned, consultants say they keep their backs straight. They might give in if preferred alternatives are not too far behind in terms of supportive evidence, impact or benefits. There are also examples where the consultant does not agree professionally with the client's preferred approach, but where the relationship with the client is given most weight.

The second source of pressure on the independence of advice comes from personal relationships with a client that may arise during the assignment, or that already existed before the assignment. Examples are getting drunk together, making friends and entering into a love affair. In the case of an existing friendship, an example is the request for help with improving business operations, including ending a practice of tax evasion. Phasing out this illegal practice means consultants commit to such practices for friends, while they would not be willing to do so otherwise.

Illustrative Jokes Related to professional independence and client influence the selected jokes address several issues with objectivity and professional judgement. It is a more subtle kind of joking than in the earlier jokes, but again integrity standards are activated as being violated.

From: Consulting Revisited

- In case of doubt, make it sound convincing.
- If you consult enough experts, you can confirm any opinion.

(http://nowthatisfunny.blogspot.com/2005/10/jokes-about-consultants.html)

From: Consultant or Prostitute?

- Creating fantasies for your clients is rewarded.

(www.caseinterview101.blogspot.com/2014/04/how-big-4-employees-are-like-prostitutes.html)

Interpretation The selected jokes criticize aspects of the consultant-client relationship, and how clients can manipulate consultants. The last line in "consulting revisited" is quite telling: clients know how to get the outcomes they want. Also, sexual relationships between consultants and clients are addressed in several jokes, with consultants in a more dependent position again. When independence is an issue, character is criticized, which makes the criticism foremost virtue ethical. Independence is a key value in the Dutch code of conduct, though not in the FEACO code. The jokes are written in the second person and read like insider jokes, addressing where and how consultants feel themselves that they are crossing the line of independence.

3. **Overbilling, and Selling Juniors as Seniors**

   Often consultants know up front they cannot deliver everything they promise in their proposal. Still, they pretend they can when closing the deal and they suggest in the contract they will do more and spend more hours than they are really planning to do. This starts during proposal writing. Junior consultants report how their CVs have been pimped in the proposal to support a higher fee. Next to that, juniors often execute work that, according to the proposal, was intended for a senior. Although contracts usually indicate that the project team cannot be guaranteed, junior consultants have to walk on their toes in such cases. Both clients and junior employees experience the consequences of such overbilling.

Illustrative Jokes The selected jokes below illustrate how consultancies are billing more hours than they deliver, and also that partners drop all kinds of tasks on the desk of juniors they are not yet qualified to do.

> **St. Peter**
>
> A contractor dies on in a fishing accident on his 40th birthday and finds himself greeted at the Pearly Gates by a brass band. Saint Peter runs over, shakes his hand and says "Congratulations!"
>
> "Congratulations for what?" asks the contractor.
>
> "Congratulations for what?" says Saint Peter. "We are celebrating the fact that you lived to be 160 years old."
>
> "But that's not true", says the consultant. "I only lived to be forty."
>
> "That's impossible", says Saint Peter, "we added up your time sheets."
>
> (www.infolanka.com/jokes/messages/1581.html)

> A Partner in a large consulting firm and a more junior colleague decide to go on a weekend trip hunting bears.
>
> They arrive at their small log cabin set in a clearing deep in the forest. The Junior Consultant starts to prepare a simple meal for them in the kitchen and begins to set up the range of equipment he has brought along for the bear hunt.
>
> The Partner drops his bags and immediately disappears out the front door of the cabin; he is gone for about an hour.
>
> Suddenly, the Partner comes running at full speed out of the trees, back across the clearing and straight in through the front door of the cabin, with a huge grizzly bear just a few paces behind him.
>
> As he disappears out the back door he yells over his shoulder at the Consultant *"OK, You skin this Beauty, I'll go get us another!"*
>
> (www.reddit.com/r/consulting/comments/5xpwbz/best_jokes_about_consultants/).

Interpretation The first joke criticizes the practice of overbilling which is clearly unethical from a deontological and virtue ethical perspective. The criticism is linked to the codes of conduct where reliability is at stake as contracts are not transparent, and consultants do not live up to them. In the second joke, the bear represents a new assignment, and the partner is doing what you could call acquisition, while the junior is left to kill and skin the bear, which means executing a very difficult assignment, without senior colleagues that can support. It is a common experience among juniors, and their interests are harmed. If they cannot manage, clients will feel the consequences as well. Given the intimate knowledge expressed in the jokes they read like insider jokes, and they illustrate quite well a very common kind of problem that both clients and juniors may encounter.

4. **Fake It Till You Make It**

    Overbilling is a form of dishonesty, and so is bluffing related to expertise. Consultants often suggest more experience and knowledge than they really have. It almost seems a second nature of consultants that they overpromise and try to catch up during the assignment. They learn while getting paid by the client, and consultants tell with great pride how this usually works out by investing many extra hours, and working very hard. However, junior consultants also report how they struggle and feel insecure. Sometimes they become a project manager without any experience, or they give a workshop on digitization without sufficient knowledge. Then they have to fall back on the formula: "good question, we'll come back to that later". Others had to replace a senior manager during a board meeting at the client's site due to a car breakdown and did the best they could. What also happens is that consultancies take on more projects than capacity allows for. Usually, a few proposed projects are cancelled, but sometimes all of them start, which creates capacity problems. In one case, a consultancy never did a similar assignment before, still claiming they were qualified, and the client accepted. Consultants have also agreed on 'milestones' in the contract they knew they could never achieve, hoping for a good overall ending. Mostly, the bluffing works out well, but sometimes the hidden risks for clients are really high. Consultants seem to pay the price for such bluffing, as they have to make up for their lack of knowledge and expertise with overtime and extra engagement.

Illustrative Jokes There are many jokes in the sample related to lack of expertise. The fake it till you make it practice means that expertise can be matched in the course of the assignment. Selected jokes illustrate how consequences of this practice spill over into work-life conflicts, given the huge time investments that are demanded to live up to the bluffing:

From: Top Ten Ways to Know You've Got the Consulting Bug

- Constant urge to give advice on subjects you know nothing about.
- A two-page story in Business Week is all it takes to make you an expert.
- Firmly believe that an objective viewpoint means more than any real work experience.
- Tired of having a social life beyond work.

(www.organisationalpsychology.nz/_content/_jokes/isconsultants.html)

Wife or Mistress

A lawyer, a doctor and a management consultant were discussing the relative merits of having a wife or a mistress.

The lawyer says: "For sure a mistress is better. If you have a wife and want to divorce, there are a number of complex legal problems to resolve and it will probably be very expensive."

The doctor says: "It's better to have a wife because the sense of security and wellbeing lowers your stress and your blood pressure and is good for your health."

The management consultant says: "You're both wrong. It's best to have both, so that when your wife thinks you're with your mistress, and your mistress thinks you're with your wife—you can go to the office and get some work done."

(https://managementconsulted.com/about/consulting-jokes/)

Interpretation The first joke indicates that expertise lacks when consultants start or sell an assignment. Both jokes illustrate how consultants are willing to go the extra mile, which is needed when you start projects without sufficient expertise. Consultants pay the price in terms of reduced private life, due to the overly high work demands. In the fake it till you make it category, a project ends well for the client, due to the massive learning investments made by consultants. From a consequentialist perspective, no harm is done to the client. Still, consultants do operate in the grey zones of their codes of conduct related to expertise. Maybe they would argue they have the experience and skills to catch up in time. Therefore, virtue ethics best helps to criticize this behaviour, as consultants are not honest with their clients. They are even reckless, as they take risks a client would not like them to take. Jokes are written in the second person, which makes sense, as outsiders will not notice what risks they have been subject to. Accordingly, these are insider jokes.

5. **Extending Unnecessary Work: A Revenue Model**
   Consultants sometimes continue with assignments that will lead nowhere, especially in change projects. The client wants to pay, but consultants feel useless. For example, in one case, consultants gave their clients a sense of security after an IT migration by just staying, in case something might go wrong. A big team of consultants did nothing for weeks. Another example is a customer who wanted to implement a change process against the will of the involved employees. How long do you go on with that, very well knowing the project is going to fail in the end? Or, in preparation for a change process consultants made an analysis with suggestions for a roadmap, while the will to change was insufficient from the start. Completing such assignments provides revenues, but generates very little added value. These projects are carried out until the end, or even stretched at the expense of clients. However, when clients ask for this, it is tempting to suggest you feel their problem and to propose you can help.

   Illustrative Jokes Many business jokes in the sample picture consultants earning money without really helping clients or without adding much value. The selected jokes criticize this reality in different ways.

   > It takes two things to be a consultant—grey hair and hemorrhoids. The grey hair makes you look distinguished and the hemorrhoids make you look concerned.
   > (www.pinterest.com/pin/280560251758981648/)

   > What do consultants when they see light at the end of the tunnel? Sell more tunnel.
   > (tunnel joke based on: https://maaw.info/GadgetsandGames/PoliticalJokes.htm, joke 34)

   > From: Top Ten Things a Consultant Shouldn't Tell a Client.
   >
   > - I could just tell you the answer, but we're committed to a three-month project.
   >
   > (www.mycustomer.com/marketing/strategy/top-ten-things-a-consultant-shouldnt-tell-a-client)

Interpretation Jokes like these suggest consultants extend projects within the scope of a contract, also if they could have sold the solution in less time. It is part of their business model to be opportunistic. The jokes show a critical first-person voice (insider perspective) and a "third-person" outsider perspective. It seems the practice is noticed by clients. The ethical perspectives to criticize the behaviour is mostly virtue ethics, indicated by feelings of uneasiness on the side of the consultants that work on the project. Still, the more senior consultants responsible for the deal feel they operate within the contract, and also the codes leave sufficient room for this practice. A consequentialist form of critique would consider the impact on clients, but as they often co-create the problem, consultants merely exploit the opportunities.

6. **Confidentiality and Double Billing**

    Consultants usually sign for keeping all client information confidential. Competitors of their own clients should never find out about strategies and practices by them as consultants. Nevertheless, consultants do want to exploit the accumulated knowledge and experience they gain during their assignments. Capitalizing on such knowledge and experience can lead to various dilemmas. For instance, can you write proposals based on previous projects, can you carry out projects strongly inspired by previous work and what about reselling solutions that have already been developed for another client? The first customer that paid for a solution is the owner, while the consultants still have the solution and want to resell it. Consultants have reported that a whole CRS (central reservation system) is sold a second time, after some minor adjustments. Systems developed for the financial sector were said to be sold several times as well. In addition, knowledge about a large customer with dominant market positions is almost impossible to anonymize. Consultants, therefore, find it difficult to work with their strict non-disclosure agreements, and they often bend the rules without sharing this practice with their clients. Towards the client, this is not very reliable, and the customer who paid first might disagree, when informed about such a practice of double billing. Consultants know they cross the line of confidentiality, but as long as no one notices and their clients stay happy, they take the risk.

    Illustrative Jokes Breach of confidentiality is not criticized very much in consultant jokes, probably because it should not be noticed. Still, one joke in the sample is quite hard on consultants' unreliability. Double billing is somewhat better illustrated in the jokes, but without the fine nuances.

    > A Mexican bandit made a specialty of crossing the Rio Grande from time to time and robbing banks in Texas. Finally, a reward was offered for his capture, and an enterprising Texas ranger decided to track him down. After a lengthy search, he traced the bandit to his favourite cantina, snuck up behind him, put his trusty six-shooter to the bandit's head, and said, "You are under arrest. Tell me where you hid the loot or I'll blow your brains out." But the bandit didn't speak English, and the Ranger didn't speak Spanish. Fortunately, a bilingual consultant was in the saloon and translated the Ranger's message. The terrified bandit blurted out, in Spanish, that the loot was buried under the oak tree in back of the cantina. "What did he say?"

asked the Ranger. The consultant answered, "He said Get lost, Gringo. You wouldn't dare shoot me."

(www.sucs.swan.ac.uk/~cmckenna/humour/work/consult.html).

Top Ten Things You'll Never Hear from your Consultant

(1)   You're right; we're billing way too much for this.

(http://nowthatisfunny.blogspot.com/2005/10/jokes-about-consultants.html)

While confidentiality issues and reselling are a big theme in the illustrations provided by consultants in interviews, related jokes remain somewhat superficial here. They more address consultants' opportunism and money-earning focus. Confidentiality remains an implied theme. The jokes also read more like outsider jokes. That makes sense, as consultants may have an interest in hiding. It even is an obligation given the confidentiality agreements in their contracts. Still, the double billing practice also violates confidentiality and reliability principles in codes of conduct. The practice can be criticized based on these principles by taking a deontological stance. The practice translates into character as well. However, from a consequentialist perspective consultants seem able to keep the consequences for clients under control.

7. **Supporting Morally Dirty Clients**

    Consultants sometimes accept clients with a dubious reputation, an agenda that is not sustainable with practices close to being illegal. It is not the most frequently mentioned issue in the interviews, but in terms of moral impact, it creates very problematic situations for the involved consultants. Some even decide to quit their jobs, in other cases, they try to turn things towards the better, and some accept and go with the flow. For instance, one client is strongly committed to the use of fossil fuels, while the consultant sees absolutely no future here. His way out is to help make the energy mix more sustainable. Another consultant worked for a client who did not want to spend money on the necessary protection of privacy-sensitive data. He chose to address the issue, but leaves it at that. Also in a project to develop e-Health solutions the privacy of patients was insufficiently protected. Consultants could not do much here either, given the budget constraints. Very challenging was an issue for a consultant who had to help a client develop a 'dual-use' technology (which can be used for both civil and military purposes), knowing that this client would most likely use the technology for dubious military actions. In another extreme case, a major European transport organization asked for help in avoiding liability for accidents, caused by overtired bus drivers employed by sub-contractors of the client. The aim of the project was to find the loopholes in the law so that these profitable but dangerous practices could continue. The consultant in question raised the unethical side of these practices with his own management and with the client, and was told that the subcontractor practices were indeed operating in a grey zone, but that it was not illegal. This was the reason for the consultant to end the relationships with his employer. While consultants can find themselves in a very uncomfortable position here with such employers and clients, the client's stakeholders seem the biggest victims here.

Illustrative jokes Working for clients with a questionable moral agenda is articulated in insider jokes that compare consultants with prostitutes. When looking at the lines on clients and employers in the selected list of jokes from the sample, their roles are strongly criticized.

> From: Consultant or prostitute?
>
> - You are not proud of what you do.
> - You are embarrassed to tell people what you do for a living.
> - If a client beats you up, the pimp just sends you to another client.
> - Even though you might get paid the big bucks, it's the client who walks away smiling
>
> (www.organisationalpsychology.nz/_content/_jokes/isconsultants.html)
>
> A consultant is someone who comes in to solve a problem and stays around long enough to become part of it.
>
> (www.ronspace.org/consult.htm).

Interpretation Working for morally dirty clients has a big impact on consultants. Consultants can feel like prostitutes and make jokes about their vulnerability. In these insider jokes, the pains of consultants are articulated, not the pains of the victims of their dirty clients. The presented jokes mostly indicate virtue ethical problems experienced in the consultant-client relationship, making consultants feel heartless and irresponsible. There certainly is a consequentialist side to the problem when looking at the client's stakeholders, which is more illustrated by the second joke. Consultants become partners in crime, operate in a legal grey zone, and their codes will not support this. Many principles are violated here, but mostly meticulousness. Jokes address some of the issues, but in a more generic, associative way. The interviews show what is really going on, and are needed to be able to see what is really behind these jokes.

8. **Underperformance**

    Sometimes consultants take overly big risks when the gap between their expertise and client demands feels unbridgeable. When discussing the proposal with clients they openly indicate capacity problems, lack of expertise or insufficient turnaround time. The fake it till you make it approach seems out of scope. Sometimes the assignment is still given by the client and accepted by the consultancy. Consultants working on such assignments experience major problems. While the client might think any help is welcome, poor performance and big mistakes are the results. Consultants report to be open about their failures and try over again, but when skills are lacking not with a better result. Others report they fear their mistakes will only show later. An example is a conversion of insurance contracts during an IT migration, in which conditions for some insured parties deteriorated unnoticed due to standardization.

2.3 Application—Ten Business Ethical Transgressions Illustrated

Another example is a large-scale evaluation of clients of a bank in connection with new legislation on money laundering and tax evasion. In these very big assignments, hundreds of junior consultants do the work. Many feel they are not up to the task and suspect they might wrongly give clearance to customers, or wrongly block their accounts. The consequences for clients' clients can be considerable, and consultants struggle with their conscience.

Illustrative Jokes Several jokes picture consultants' incompetence. That you can only accept assignments with sufficient competence is stressed in all codes of conduct worldwide, Still, bad examples abound, and in jokes selected from the sample underperformance is indicated like this:

> "What is the difference between a consultant and a cable car?
>
> The cable car stops when it loses track!"
>
> (Cope, 2003, p. 1;
>
> https://books.google.nl/books?id=__kAIKcBlwMC&printsec=frontcover&dq=seven+c%27s+of+consulting&hl=nl&sa=X&redir_esc=y#v=onepage&q=seven%20c's%20of%20consulting&f=false)

> **Consultant Brains**
>
> In a village in darkest Africa a sign hung over a Headhunter's market stall:
>
> - Ordinary brains $10 /lb
> - Engineer brains $8 /lb
> - Doctor brains $7 /lb
> - Accountant brains $15 /lb
> - Consultant brains $114 /lb
>
> Asked to explain the relatively high cost of consultant brains, the head hunter said "You don't appreciate how many consultants we have to catch to get a pound of brains!"
>
> (www.ronspace.org/consult.htm).

Interpretation The selected jokes criticize consultants' lack of competence from different angles. While consultants say they are explicit about their limitations, they still accept assignments they are not qualified for. Consultants in this situation indicate they feel guilty, try a second time, spend a lot of unpaid work and still cannot make the client happy. This is illustrated in the cable car joke. They also appear as incompetent more structurally and this hurts their reputation as illustrated in the brains joke. The jokes have virtue ethical implications. However, not only consultants themselves can feel how the expertise principle is violated and how their character is harmed. This is also visible to outsiders. Consistent with the observable consequences of underperformance, the jokes are written as outsider jokes, using the third person.

9. **Insufficient Protection of Client Data**

Consultants experience it as a challenge to adequately protect sensitive client data during assignments. Consultants do their work on laptops and colleagues can easily look over their shoulder in an office garden, and so can strangers when they work in a cafe. What is more, if the laptop is left unattended in the train, in a café or at the office, it is very easy to steal. Consultants get extensive training in how to protect data, but some of the protocols highly interfere with normal social rules. Consultants want to be able to trust their colleagues and do not like to take their laptop to the bathroom as standard procedure. However, when things go wrong, it mostly is not as expected: a laptop was stolen from someone's hands, or a young colleague was placing confidential project information on a personal website for CV building. In these two cases, consultants have shared the problem openly with their client, and no real damage was done. Another example is from a consultant who left his laptop together with confidential printouts unattended in a bag in the open office, after leaving for home with a headache, that resulted in a serious talk with his manager. Such sloppiness is not appreciated, and several company rules were violated.

Illustrative Jokes The many rules for protecting client data are rather new due to the new ways of working, and the sample does not have much jokes on data protection procedures. Only some jokes in the sample illustrate the challenges that come with data protection like creating the right passwords, or keeping your laptop close.

> A female computer consultant is helping a smug man set up his machine. She asks him what password he'd like to log on with. Wanting to embarrass the woman, he tells her to enter the word PENIS. Without saying a thing, she keys in the password and almost dies laughing at the computer's reply: PASSWORD REJECTED—NOT LONG ENOUGH.
>
> (www.jokebuddha.com/Consultant/recent/3).
>
> From: **You know you've been a consultant for too long when…**
>
> - You feel naked without a laptop hanging from your left shoulder
>
> (http://sunflowersamurai2008.blogspot.com/2008/02/you-know-youve-been-consultant-for-too.html)

Interpretation As the topic of data protection is getting more attention recently, it will probably figure more in future jokes. The selected jokes illustrate the practice of keeping your laptop close, to protect client data. Easy passwords are criticized, but good passwords are a memory challenge not everyone is up to. Criticisms in jokes are foremost criticizing the many rules and principles that should prevent data leaks and the related struggles with complying. It makes the jokes insider jokes currently, as the biggest problem for consultants seems following many impractical rules. From an ethics perspective, various logics are clashing, like being a trusting colleague and taking sufficient care of data protection (conflicting virtues). Still, criminality that makes use of badly protected data is growing, and the potential harm is substantial.

10. **Bending Conclusions**
Consultants are masters of framing conclusions in such a way that a client likes them. Usually, they stay within the limits of the available evidence. However, sometimes consultants make mistakes in their calculations, and when clients then like the outcomes, it is difficult to correct them. In one case, a company is valued on the basis of a programme that assesses working capital. However, the valuation is very high. The consultants suspect the programme has an error, but they do not succeed in finding it. Only after the company has been sold at too high a price, the error comes to light. So what then? The buyer was at a disadvantage, the consultant can no longer do anything because of confidentiality, and the client is happy with the outcome. In another case of selling a company, a consultant spots an error in how the value of the company is calculated, and she addresses the failure, even though her client would benefit if she did not. The mistake is too obvious though. However, when doing negotiations, valuation gets more flexible, and her game is different. Another example is estimating the profitability of a particular kind of renewable energy. It is a sustainable form of energy, so a high estimate is attractive to both the environment, the environmental consultant and the client. But how far can you go? Overall, desirable answers are gladly given, accepting a fairly wide margin of error.

Illustrative Jokes A couple of consultant jokes focus on consultants' use of euphemisms, their flexibility in using evidence and their framing tactics.

> From: **Consultants Commandments**
>
> - If at first you don't succeed, destroy all evidence that you tried.
> - For every action, there is an equal and opposite criticism.
>
> (www.kilvo.org/humour/consultants-commandments/)
>
> From: **You Might Be a Consultant if...**
>
> - You can explain the difference between "down-sizing," "right-sizing," and "firing people's arses," and you actually believe your explanation.
>
> (http://nowthatisfunny.blogspot.com/2005/10/jokes-about-consultants.html)
>
> Santa Claus, the tooth fairy, an honest consultant and an old drunk are walking down the street together when they simultaneously spot a hundred dollar bill. Who gets it?
>
> The old drunk of course: the other three are mythical creatures.
>
> (www.organisationalpsychology.nz/_content/_jokes/isconsultants.html)

Interpretation That in these jokes the honest consultant is seen as a mythical creature, that evidence of failure can be removed and that any option can always be criticized all indicate a great flexibility in presenting facts. The first two jokes are clearly insider jokes, and the latter feels the same, although the narrative is of a different kind. An ethical angle that fits the criticism in these jokes is virtue ethics, as consultants seem not entirely comfortable with their practices. They translate into character, especially their independence. It is a balancing act where they seem to cross the line more often than they consider acceptable. The seriousness of the issues can also be assessed from a consequentialist angle. In the interviews, consequences are critical in some of the given illustrations. Compared to these illustrations, the jokes are again quite generic. They need the examples to come to life.

2.3.3 Jokes-Based Illustrations and Their Contributions to Ethical Research Questions

When considering the added value of the presented jokes-based illustration method, the illustrations generate descriptive knowledge related to how the ten transgressions look like, or how consultants do this, similar to a normal illustration. However, the jokes illustrating the top ten do not provide an exact mirror image due to irony, distortion, exaggeration, stereotyping, abstraction, etc. This type of illustration requires interpretation. What humour adds to the descriptive elements in the jokes and interviews is a normative perspective. Jokes stress the feeling of absurdity in the illustrated situation, that is, when a reader feels the joke is indeed illustrative of the unethical aspect of the described practice and does fit.

When reflecting on what kinds of unethical practices are illustrated, we see how most jokes relate to virtue ethical concerns, and how they stay close to consultants themselves as insider jokes. The illustrated transgressions relate to character, and they have a more permanent manifestation. They are best visible to consultants themselves. Examples are "lack of independence", "overly extending projects" and "supporting morally dirty clients". Here, consultants take limited responsibility for stakeholder interest. "Fake it till you make it" and "bending conclusions' also link to character: consultants are not being honest or are overly risk-taking. The existence of various public jokes indicates the behaviour is normal or common to some extent, and part of professional routines. Therefore, we can conclude that jokes are very well able to pinpoint transgressions with a virtue ethical character, that makes them useful for illustrating issues of professional ethics more generally.

Some of the other issues in the top ten are criticized from an outsider's perspective due to their visible and damaging consequences such as "harming interests of client employees", or visible "underperformance". This translates into consequentialist critiques. Visibility is lower when norms or contracts are violated as with "overbilling and selling juniors as seniors", "confidentiality and repeat business" or "insufficient protection of client data". However, if clients would find out, the impact on consultants is big due to the legal consequences. As many consultants move over to clients after some years, secretive practices may get noticed at some point. Still, the consequences for clients seem mostly not too bad yet—that would harm consultants' own business in the end. More generally, we can conclude that critical business jokes are also able to illustrate ethical transgressions with a consequentialist or deontological character, even though vices seem to have most fun potential.

The illustrative contributions of jokes make them a descriptive instrument with some limitations due to irony, distortion, abstraction, etc., as well as a means to stimulate normative judgement, and activate moral standards. This dual ability helps not only to illustrate empirically grounded arguments such as the top ten ethical transgressions in consulting but also to illustrate theoretically argued transgressions. Most relevant for business ethics seems to be the jokes' normative call that triggers the laughing emotion. This is the real added value of the jokes-based illustration method. That makes the method useful in answering evaluative research questions about ethical transgressions. Adding business jokes as illustration to a result helps to answer questions like *what* are common ethical transgressions in a business field, and *why* these are transgressions. It is the ability of humour to activate norms, to indicate that there is an ethical issue, and why it is an issue.

2.4 Possibilities and Limitations of Jokes as Illustrations

2.4.1 Jokes Can Illustrate Common Unethical Business Behaviours

Common ethical transgressions that consultants have shared in interviews can all be illustrated by business jokes on consultants. Each of the top ten ethical transgressions has been addressed. As the level of detail in jokes is limited compared to the real-life case narratives, they cannot give away all details of professional life. Still, related to the context outlined in the interviews, the jokes make perfect sense. The more common an unethical practice is, as indicated in Table 2.2, the better the jokes illustrate the transgression, and the more business jokes are made in the business context, and thus available to choose from.

The consultant jokes selected for illustration, trigger expectations of what we consider acceptable or desirable practices, while at the same time showing how these common expectations are violated. By provoking a feeling of emotional absurdity, as indicated by Veatch (1998), jokes can be a perfect articulation of moral judgement. They activate moral standards in a humorous way. At the same time, to make the joke understandable, the illustrated immoral behaviours should be familiar enough to be recognizable to a wider audience and to meet the normality condition of humour. That means, the audience should be able to feel: indeed, this does happen and it is emotionally absurd due to its immorality.

Some issues in the top ten unethical behaviour seem consultant specific such as the theme of overlooking wider client and stakeholder interests (Krehmeyer & Freeman, 2012; Poulfelt, 1997; Schein, 1997; Sturdy, 2009). Other themes relate to professional service firms more generally. Lack of expertise (Bouwmeester & Stiekema, 2015) is such a broader theme. The brains joke, for instance, mentions other professions with under-average brain volumes (accountants). Functional dishonesty like bluffing, exaggeration, using euphemisms or being selective in presenting evidence is found in consulting (cf. Bouwmeester, 2013; Jackall, 1988; Redekop & Heath, 2007), but is also addressed in lawyer jokes (Galanter, 2005, p. 31–6, 157) where one-sidedness may be even stronger. The dominant sales orientation and overcharging (O'Mahoney, 2011; Sturdy, 1997) also figure in lawyer jokes (Galanter, 2005, p. 64), as well as exploitation of juniors by their management (Bouwmeester & Kok, 2018; Galanter, 2005, p. 183). Many ethical issues addressed in the consultant jokes have wider business relevance, and there are also many more business jokes available, than only on consultants. This makes the jokes-based illustration method applicable to other professional service firms, as well as wider fields of business ethics.

How do I select the right jokes for illustration? The topical fit of the jokes is key when searching and selecting jokes for illustration. Jokes can often be read in different ways, they carry ambiguity, irony, abstraction, emphasis, etc., and they always need interpretation to mitigate representation bias. Jokes usually do not provide an exact mirror image of a situation, but emphasize elements. Therefore, the joke's topical fit with the ethical issue has to be carefully considered. Selecting part of a list joke is a way to make the topical fit stronger, by leaving out from a list joke lines that are irrelevant. How well jokes as illustration may work, can be experienced in this chapter by assessing the strength of illustrations of various top ten transgressions. Selection requires an aesthetic judgement by the author. Next to joke selection, joke interpretation is important to make an illustration work. To get the joke, it does require a sense of humour and some context knowledge on the side of the researchers/authors, as well as on the side of the readers. Checking the illustrative value of jokes with some others may help to select the better option.

How can I help the audience to get the joke? To be of value as illustration, audiences confronted with jokes on business ethical issues need sufficient context knowledge to be able to understand such jokes, and to interpret them well. Workplace humour as it unfolds in daily practice is mostly only funny for those who participate in the joking. Such jokes are bound to time, place and social context. Internet jokes have a wider reach, and aim at wider audiences. Still, when using jokes to illustrate business behaviours, audiences need to have sufficient experience with the profession, the business or the criticized practice to understand the humour of the joke, and its implied critical message. If you cannot assume this, it is advisable to provide such context knowledge before presenting the joke. By illustrating the top ten with empirical interview findings, this context knowledge has been provided. When illustrating theoretical arguments it could help to give different kinds of illustrations, both traditional and joke based.

2.4.2 Method Limitations of Using Jokes as Illustration of Ethical Transgressions

The discussed illustration possibilities of jokes have application potential in three other research methods in business ethics: jokes-based interviews, surveys and content analysis. However, before turning to these other methods we have to acknowledge some limitations based on how well consultant jokes could illustrate the top ten ethical transgressions in this field. These limitations need to be considered when assessing the illustrative potential of jokes when moving to other jokes-based research methods and to wider business contexts. When using the jokes-based illustration method it is important to understand that this illustration method always serves as an addition to an empirically or theoretically founded result, and as such the jokes-based illustration method always implies a mixed method design.

The illustrative potential of jokes first depends on how common or rare an immoral practice is, second on how visible norm violation becomes (in vices, negative consequences or harmed principles) and third on how funny immoral behaviour can be (which excludes extreme transgressions). In addition, immoral use of jokes due to stereotyping effects needs to be prevented.

To begin with, only more general and more common issues will make it into the jokes. The transgressions should be able to meet the normality condition of jokes so that sufficient people within the targeted audiences will recognize the unethical behaviours. Compared to the issues discussed in all 126 interviews, the top 10 covers most of the mentioned issues (see Table 2.2). Very unique experiences will not make it into jokes published on the Internet. They might be joking material in individual work settings though. What we can also observe is that jokes in the top five are better for illustration than jokes on issues that have been mentioned less often, which must be due to the normality condition. They seem also more to the point and more developed. Therefore, the more common the ethical issue, the better public jokes may illustrate the transgression.

Second virtue ethical criticisms were most prominent in the interviews with consultants, and they relate well to insider jokes. Coping humour is a good way to reflect on unethical behaviours you struggle with in your work, and to make them discussable. This is first and foremost something that can happen within the occupation, and consultants themselves are the best audience to understand such insider jokes. For outsiders, these moral character struggles are not as visible, and maybe also not as funny. For them, jokes that criticize consequences are more imaginative. Clients and their employees can relate to projects that fail, and they see how consultants underperform. When it comes to deontological issues jokes may become less illustrative and less detailed. The reliability jokes, for instance, hint at practices that require a secretive approach that insiders will hide for outsiders. Still, the data protection jokes allow for a more open discussion, where some of the rules can be ridiculed as well.

Third, there might be humour bias related to what issues are funny. Bad character seems to inspire joking, bad luck and bad consequences do as well, but breaking moral rules might be less funny when it is no mild offense anymore. Also, when it comes to severe consequences some jokes might turn into hate jokes, and then trigger anger as emotion instead of amusement. When behaviours tend to become criminal, at some point we cannot laugh anymore. Jokes are thus bound to the mild offence of moral norms, excluding the more serious unethical behaviours that journalists report. Still, illustrative jokes have shown to be complementary to the more critical and extreme case reports of journalists. In addition, jokes tend to critique, not to compliment. That is a limitation as well.

Fourth, jokes could contribute to stereotyping, which is a form of overgeneralization. When considering jokes-based illustrations, the fact that audiences get the joke and thus may recognize consultant behaviours, should not support interpretations that all consultants double bill, overcharge, fake it till they make it, etc. The risk that jokes are stereotyping, needs to be taken care of. It very much depends on the ethics of the writer if a joke will become tendentious (Billig, 2005; Zaldivar, 2021). To avoid this, it is important to keep distance when using public jokes for illustration. It is a joke that is made and shared, it is not a joke of the researcher or ethics scholar. We need to handle sharp jokes with care, just like sharp knives, or words.

2.4.3 Reviewer Perspectives on Jokes-Based Illustrations and Possible Responses

The method of illustrating empirical or theoretical arguments with text jokes or cartoons is a way jokes have been used in research before. That means, illustrative use of jokes has survived reviewer criticism. It is a rhetorical device that might help to strengthen an argument in terms of relevance and visibility. Jokes may also have uses beyond illustrating ethical critique, such as indicating low status (cf. Fincham, 1999, p. 341).

Illustration is recommended in theory papers (Sutton and Staw, 1995). Still, as illustrative jokes can be very narrowly focused in their message, potentially including stereotyping, and very often exaggeration or distortion, adding the researcher's interpretation to the humorous material is advisable. Maybe not always, as Schneider and Sting (2020) have an illustrative cartoon on the front page of their article, as if it were a book cover. That one is self-explanatory and goes without author interpretations. The article itself also provides sufficient context and background to make sense of why the joke is selected. In other cases, however, reviewers might question the relevance of the jokes-based illustration, or criticize the implied morality of a joke itself. Some jokes have been experienced as unethical or off limits by particular audiences, as happened with several Mohamed cartoons.

It is good to check with some readers if they feel the humorous illustrations add value, and if they can see a topical connection. This helps increasing intercoder reliability, and reviewers will like that. I asked for such feedback for this book as well (see my acknowledgements), and in some cases I changed the introduction to a joke to give more context, or worked on the interpretation, to help readers to see what I see.

2.4.4 Practical Tips for Searching Critical Business Jokes

For finding critical business jokes that illustrate unethical behaviour in a profession, a search on google like: jokes/cartoon/memes AND consultants/bankers/managers/politicians/tobacco, etc., will generate some first results for the profession of interest. More specific words related to the issue can be added, but also effective is to search within a more general sample for specific issues, or do more specific searches within websites with their own search option. When extensive sampling is done, and a maximum is reached, selection of the best illustrative jokes is the next step.

Some general sites are useful for searching within the site for the profession or type of business you are interested in. They offer business jokes, and within them you can search for a particular content (all sites last accessed August 8, 2021):

- www.workjoke.com
- www.jokes.one
- www.jokebuddha.com
- www.jokelabs.com/humor-jokes-cat-15-profession-jokes.html
- www.nowthatisfunny.blogspot.com
- www.officehumorblog.com/index.php/category/office-jokes/
- http://www.officediversions.com (navigation pane just above the first photo, where you can select a profession like consultants, bankers, etc.).

Cartoons can serve the same purpose, but when using cartoons copyright can be an issue. Most sites offer a search field where you can enter the profession you are interested in. Some places to find cartoons or memes are:

- www.cartoonstock.com
- www.cartooncollections.com (integrated in cartoonstock)
- www.dilbert.com
- www.knowyourmeme.com (search for profession, and then select the tab images)
- www.memegenerator.net (search for profession, then click an icon).

More tied to consultants are the sites below:

- www.organisationalpsychology.nz/_content/_jokes/isconsultants.html
- www.managementconsulted.com/about/consulting-jokes
- www.modernanalyst.com/Resources/BusinessAnalystHumor.aspx
- www.infolanka.com/jokes/messages/1581.html
- www.nowthatisfunny.blogspot.com/2005/10/jokes-about-consultants.html
- https://www.jokebuddha.com/Consultant/

- https://jokojokes.com/consultant-jokes.html (you can change consultant for banker, lawyer, researcher, etc., in the address).

  Related collections.

- https://maaw.info/GadgetsandGames/PoliticalJokes.htm
- http://homepage.tinet.ie/~nobyrne/planning_humour.html.

Acknowledgements The ten common ethical transgressions in consulting have been listed before in Bouwmeester (2020), in the Dutch professional journal *M&C Quarterly*, however, without joke illustrations or method reflections.

References

Allen, J., & Davis, D. (1993). Assessing some determinant effects of ethical consulting behavior: The case of personal and professional values. *Journal of Business Ethics, 12*(6), 449–458.

Aristoteles, O. (1985). *Nikomachische ethik*. Meiner Verlag.

Billig, M. (2005). *Laughter and ridicule: Towards a social critique of humour*. Sage.

Bouwmeester, O. (2013). Consultant jokes about managing uncertainty: Coping through humor. *International Studies of Management & Organization, 43*(3), 41–57.

Bouwmeester, O. (2020). Consultants en ethiek: Een top tien van pijnpunten. *M&C Quarterly, 2020*(2), 44–49.

Bouwmeester, O., & Kok, T. E. (2018). Moral or dirty leadership: A qualitative study on how juniors are managed in dutch consultancies. *International Journal of Environmental Research and Public Health, 15*(11), 2506.

Bouwmeester, O., & Stiekema, J. (2015). The paradoxical image of consultant expertise: A rhetorical deconstruction. *Management Decision, 53*(10), 2433–2456.

Cope, M. (2003). *The Seven Cs of consulting: The definitive guide to the consulting process*. Pearson Education.

Fincham, R. (1999). The consultant–client relationship: Critical perspectives on the management of organizational change. *Journal of Management Studies, 36*(3), 335–351.

Galanter, M. (2005). *Lowering the bar: Lawyer jokes and legal culture*. University of Wisconsin Press.

Jackall, R. (1988). *Moral mazes* (Vol. 4). Oxford University Press.

Kaptein, M., & Schwartz, M. S. (2008). The effectiveness of business codes: A critical examination of existing studies and the development of an integrated research model. *Journal of Business Ethics, 77*(2), 111–127.

Krehmeyer, D., & Freeman, R. E. (2012). Consulting and ethics. In *The Oxford Handbook of Management Consulting* (pp. 487–498). Oxford University Press.

Kubr, M. (2002). *Management consulting: A guide to the profession*. International Labour Organization.

O'Mahoney, J. (2011). Advisory anxieties: Ethical individualisation in the UK consulting industry. *Journal of Business Ethics, 104*(1), 101–113.

O'Mahoney, J., & Markham, C. (2013). *Management consultancy*. Oxford University Press.

Poulfelt, F. (1997). Ethics for management consultants. *Business Ethics: A European Review, 6*(2), 65–70.

Redekop, B. W., & Heath, B. L. (2007). A brief examination of the nature, contexts, and causes of unethical consultant behaviors. *Journal of Practical Consulting, 1*(2), 40–50.

References

Schein, E. H. (1997). The concept of "Client" from a process consultation perspective. A guide for change agents. *Journal of Organizational Change Management, 10*(3), 202–216.

Schneider, P., & Sting, F. J. (2020). Employees' perspectives on digitalization-induced change: Exploring frames of industry 4.0. *Academy of Management Discoveries, 6*(3), 406–435.

Shaw, D. (2020). Aristotle and the management consultants: Shooting for ethical practice. *Philosophy of Management, 19*(1), 21–44.

Sturdy, A. (1997). The consultancy process: An insecure business? *Journal of Management Studies, 34*(3), 389–413.

Sturdy, A. (2009). Popular critiques of consultancy and a politics of management learning? *Management Learning, 40*(4), 457.

Sutton, R. I., & Staw, B. M. (1995). What theory is not. *Administrative Science Quarterly, 40*(3) 371–384.

Thomson, J. J. (1985). The trolley problem. *Yale Law Journal, 94*(6), 1395–1415. https://doi.org/10.2307/796133

Veatch, T. C. (1998). A theory of humor. *Humor-International Journal of Humor Research, 11*(2), 161–216.

Webley, S., & Werner, A. (2008). Corporate codes of ethics: Necessary but not sufficient. *Business Ethics: A European Review, 17*(4), 405–415.

Zaldivar, E. (2021). Tendentious jokes are immoral. In J. M. Henrigillis & S. Gimbel (Eds.), *It's Funny' Cause It's True: The Lighthearted Philosophers' Society's Introduction to Philosophy through Humor* (pp. 128–134). Lighthearted Philosophers' Society. https://cupola.gettysburg.edu/oer/10/

Used Internet Sources

CBS (2021). Last accessed August 3, 2021, from https://www.cbs.nl/nl-nl/cijfers/detail/81589NED?q=702%20managmentadviesbureaus.

Consultancy.nl (2015). Last accessed August 3, 2021, from https://www.consultancy.nl/nieuws/10809/aantal-organisatieadviesbureaus-in-nl-nadert-100000.

FEACO. Last accessed December 21, 2020, from http://www.feaco.org/aboutfeaco/codeofethic.

ICM. Last accessed December 21, 2020, from https://cdn.ymaws.com/www.imcusa.org/resource/collection/FF4D824A-2E4D-4199-9263-63C5FD63D135/imc_usa_code_of_ethics__final_.pdf.

I&O Research (2019). Last accessed August 3, 2021, from https://www.ioresearch.nl/actueel/banen-in-organisatieadvies-meerderheid-werkt-zelfstandig/.

OOA/ROA. Last accessed December 21, 2020, from https://www.ooa.nl/download/?id=17939577.

Open Access This chapter is licensed under the terms of the Creative Commons Attribution 4.0 International License (http://creativecommons.org/licenses/by/4.0/), which permits use, sharing, adaptation, distribution and reproduction in any medium or format, as long as you give appropriate credit to the original author(s) and the source, provide a link to the Creative Commons license and indicate if changes were made.

The images or other third party material in this chapter are included in the chapter's Creative Commons license, unless indicated otherwise in a credit line to the material. If material is not included in the chapter's Creative Commons license and your intended use is not permitted by statutory regulation or exceeds the permitted use, you will need to obtain permission directly from the copyright holder.

Chapter 3
Critical Jokes and Moral Reflection in Interviews

3.1 Introduction to a Jokes-Based Interview Method

One of the more pressing themes in business jokes are the unethical behaviours of managers. The issue of over demanding management has been touched upon in the previously discussed top ten of business ethical transgressions under 'selling juniors for seniors' and in the 'fake it till you make it' practice, where managing consultants promise more in the contract than they should. During a project, consultants then have to put in overtime, and a lot of learning on the job. While clients are mostly satisfied with the end result, consultants, and in particular juniors have to pay by investing lots of time and effort. As in the consultant joke on bear hunting, juniors have to kill and skin the bear, while their managers only do 'acquisition'. As a result, juniors receive more work, and much more difficult work, than they should handle.

The previous chapter has shown how jokes can illustrate the most common unethical practices in business. In this chapter we turn the question around, to find out *how interview responses can illustrate and deepen the ethical issues raised in jokes, and how jokes may inspire such exploration.* Pressuring leadership in consulting is the example case used to introduce this method. The jokes-based interview method is based on open in-depth interviews that start with an invitation to reflect on jokes, in the current example study two cartoons and one text joke. The three jokes all illustrate the issue of pressuring leadership from a different angle. Interviewees are asked to interpret the jokes and to relate them to their own work experiences.

While social scientist are familiar with interview studies, for scholars in ethics this may be less common. Usually, philosophers have limited experience with empirical research methods. They may use secondary data that can be quoted, they select example cases to illustrate their argument, or use thought experiments. However, in the field of business ethics scholars are well advised to take responsibility for finding out what is going on in practice themselves, and not leave that task to journalists or social scientist only. Journalists have an interests in extreme cases. Social scientists have a broader interests but will only touch on the ethics topic incidentally. While scholars in business ethics do have a strong interest in ethics cases, their methods to explore them are very limited. Learning to do jokes-based interviews may add to their own set of useful research methods for studies in business ethics. Social scientist may benefit from the new method as well, when they need to overcome social desirability bias in their studies.

The following sections first review the state of knowledge related to pressuring leadership in consulting, to establish the pre-knowledge that can serve as standard to evaluate the findings of the new method. Then the new jokes-based interview method and the outcomes it has generated, will be discussed. The chapter concludes with the possibilities and limitations of the new jokes-based interview method, including possible reviewer concerns.

3.2 The Issue—Experiencing Overly Pressuring Leadership

The new jokes-based interview method is applied to the issue of pressuring leadership in the consulting context. What do we know about this issue based on previous studies? The consultant literature states that consultants are asked to work on average over 60 h a week in certain settings (Alvesson & Robertson, 2006; Bouwmeester et al., 2021). Promotions only occur through high commitment, and workers can feel anxious about their current status and performance (Gill, 2015, p. 309). Such factors make consulting a stressful work environment with high levels of burnout reported (Vahl, 2013, p. 8). Ultimately, society may view such negative health effects as defying morality (Skagert et al., 2008, p. 807).

However, moral criticisms on the manager-consultant relationship are less prominent in the consulting literature than criticisms related to the consultant-client relationships (cf. Allen & Davis, 1993; Poulfelt, 1997; Redekop & Heath, 2007). The latter has negative reputation effects and undermines business (Krehmeyer & Freeman, 2012, p. 87; O'Mahoney, 2011, p. 107). When it comes to the consultant-manager relationship, there are no such consequences, and many graduates even love to start working at consultancies (Rivera, 2016). Consultancies seem somehow immune to these critical judgements, or very good at neutralizing or normalizing them (Ashforth et al., 2007; Bouwmeester et al., 2021). While consulting research has identified various stressors, disturbed work-life balance and reduced employee well-being (Meriläinen et al., 2004; Mühlhaus & Bouwmeester, 2016; Noury et al., 2017; O'Mahoney, 2007), pressuring management is no big issue yet, and not addressed in codes of conduct either.

In contrast, public jokes do criticise leadership in the consulting context extensively. Leadership jokes can be found on Internet forums, in the television series House of Lies based on Kihn's (2012) novel and there are such criticisms in some autobiographical accounts of ex-consultants (i.e. O'Mahoney, 2007). Still, these criticisms do not easily surface, due to social desirability bias, career consequences, and the fact that managers and their juniors seem very skilled at normalizing such leadership behaviours. As a consequence, there seems to be a gap in our knowledge on leadership pressures due to social desirability bias.

To invite a more open reflection on morally dirty leadership in consulting as exemplary context, this chapter introduces a jokes-based interview method that starts with reflecting on jokes that illustrate pressuring leadership. The method has been developed in Bouwmeester and Kok (2018). Below the method and its outcomes will be discussed in more detail.

3.3 Application—Open Interviews and Jokes Based Reflections

3.3.1 Jokes-Based Interview Method: Start with Reflecting on Critical Business Jokes

The empirical study of ethical transgressions in business is relatively nascent. There are some interview studies, however, due to social desirability bias interviewees do not open up so easily about unethical behaviour. That also applies to consultant studies on demanding leadership roles. Discussing a topic such as pressuring leadership can be sensitive, due to feelings of shame, fear for stigma, or for career consequences. Creating rapport when discussing such sensitive topics is very important (Hermanowicz, 2002). Studying ethical transgressions in an explorative way would make a good methodological fit (Edmondson & McManus, 2007, p. 1170). Therefore, to break through barriers of social desirability bias, the proposed jokes-based interview method starts with displaying manager–employee jokes as an icebreaker, to set up the conversation and to introduce the relevant topics for an open interview.

To make it work, jokes need to be selected carefully. The purpose is to steer the conversation to morally relevant leadership issues. The two selected cartoons were found on the Internet, and illustrate different aspects of unethical leadership behaviour. The selected text joke indicates a more general dirty work experience of consultants, and work in the evenings. Such variation within the scope of the leadership topic gives interviewees room for choosing what aspects relate most to their own experiences, and what aspects they want to illustrate further. The text and the web addresses of the selected jokes can be found in Table 3.1.

The jokes-based interview method is similar to Zaltman's (1996, 1997) metaphor elicitation technique. He has used metaphors as images to learn about what consumers think of particular products or brands. In order to get the broadest possible exploration of meaning, Zaltman has suggested participants in his research to select various images themselves. The images should illustrate a brand or its meaning. When it comes to images more general, our world offers plenty of visuals with metaphorical meaning that can be selected. In contrast, there are less jokes on a topic like pressuring leadership. Therefore, we as authors have done the search in Bouwmeester and Kok

Table 3.1 Jokes used to start interviews on leadership

Cartoon and joke images, texts and web addresses
Cartoon 1: Manager A standing in the office of manager B: What are they complaining about …. The work is challenging, interesting, demanding! Manager B, sitting behind desk: AND we let them do it 80 h per week! Fran (06/07/2009) • Retrieved from: https://www.cartoonstock.com/cartoon?searchID=CS167077 • Last accessed: 26 April 2021
Cartoon 2: Male manager A to female manager B when walking through the office: Naturally our workers look happy. The penalty for not being happy is instant dismissal *Financial Times*, 20 May 2013 • Retrieved from: https://www.ft.com/content/41f990f0-b955-11e2-bc57-00144feabdc0#axz z2U2zMvxmp • Last accessed: 26 April 2021
Text joke: Please don't tell my mother I'm a consultant. She thinks I play guitar in a strip joint • Retrieved from: https://ronspace.org/consult.htm • Last accessed: 26 April 2021

(2018), and selected three jokes. The jokes-based interview method would allow for selecting more jokes, and to give respondents more options to choose from.

When showing the three jokes to the interviewees, the first cartoon generated the liveliest discussions, taking up more than half of the time of the entire interview in most cases. The second cartoon also resonated well, but interviewees came up with fewer illustrations. The text joke inspired only little discussion and was not recognized as being very illustrative for most consultants. They were mostly proud of what they did, and willing to share or tell their family and friends about their work.

My co-author has performed all interviews. She intended to become a junior consultant, and had a real interest in learning about experiences of juniors, including the perspectives of their managers. She started the interviews with a brief general introduction before showing the two cartoons and the joke, and explained that we would talk about tensions in the manager–employee relationship, but without listing the issues we had in mind. The interviewees could indicate if they recognized the messages of the jokes, and how well they illustrated what happened in their work context, given that jokes may exaggerate, include irony etc. Next the interviewer facilitated a broad discussion related to the jokes, including questions regarding over-demanding managers and being employee in such a context. Starting point were the leadership topics addressed in jokes.

To prevent that our jokes-based interview questions would become leading (Alvesson, 2003, p. 20), interviewees could talk about the cartoon they considered most relevant, and they could freely associate, illustrate with related experiences, elaborate or add nuance. The interviewer asked follow-up questions related to the experiences and memories that were shared. In this process the text joke got little attention. Therefore, when a joke does not resonate well with experiences, it hardly leads to results. In this case the strip joint joke also seems to be too generic, and not sufficiently related to the topic of leadership.

Interviewees were 12 managers and for each of them one of their junior employees. This dyadic approach secured we could hear the story from two sides. The 24 Interviews lasted an average of 45 min, ranging from 30 to 60 min. We offered anonymity, requested permission to record, and transcribed all interviews. Interviews have been analysed based on open and axial coding (Corbin & Strauss, 1990; Gioia et al., 2013). The next section illustrates the approach for the first cartoon (see Fig. 3.1), by showing the kind of responses it has helped to generate.

3.3.2 Interview Results Show Recognition, Nuancing, and Going Beyond the Cartoon

Confirming and Nuancing When interviewees started reflecting on the Fran (2009) cartoon, the interpretations from both junior 7 and manager 12 indicated it is quite common in consulting to be asked to work up to 60 h a week and incidentally also up to 80 h a week:

> Yes, juniors work long hours. There are projects where they work for longer periods about 60 h a week.—Manager 12.
>
> Consulting is working from deadline to deadline. And if a deadline requires a lot, then working 80 h occurs easily.—Junior 7.

Most responses indicated that consultants work substantially longer than the Dutch legal maximum of 40 h a week, but also less than 80 h on average. The cartoon requires interpretation to understand that the 80 h is common but not average:

> I understand that cartoon saying we work 80 h, but it is exaggerated. Who is working 80 h …?—Junior 1.

We can thus see respondents don't feel pushed to agree with the cartoon. They seem to know the genre invites interpretation. Still, because projects have overlapping deadlines, and consultant face pressuring managers and demanding clients, junior 11 confirms the cartoon by comparing his work environment to a "pressure cooker":

> Working here is working in a pressure cooker. It is just hard work. You have deadlines.—Junior 11.

Managers make the pressures as high as the juniors indicate. Junior 10 for instance *laughs* while looking at the cartoon:

> This is anonymous? Yes, this applies to my manager! This is quite bad indeed. But I need to add some nuance. I recognize this, but it is also something I want to do. I chose to work the 60, 70, 80 h. And I seek challenges, new clients, personal development, etc. This works bi-directional.—Junior 10.

The manager rhetoric in the cartoon is thus taken up on by junior 10. The challenges and the interesting work are seen as motivating as suggested in the cartoon, whereas at the same time the long workweeks up to 80 h are also felt as something quite bad.

Fig. 3.1 Cartoon illustrating pressuring leadership. www.CartoonStock.com

3.3 Application—Open Interviews and Jokes Based Reflections

Further Elaborations The cartoon sparks recognition and some nuancing, but also inspires further associations beyond the direct message. For instance, in what way leadership is demanding is not only a matter of work hours. It also comes with a competitive work culture:

> Consulting is a hard environment. As a junior you have to satisfy your project managers. Failing to satisfy your manager can only happen 1 or 2 times. Then they look for someone else.—Manager 9

Not only managers need to be satisfied, also clients. That is what managers try to accomplish when juniors feel they are overly demanding:

> The key rule is: as long as the client is happy. And that can be a really dangerous criterion, in which you can easily go too far.[…] If you […] want to do everything perfectly, working as a consultant is not sustainable. And that's what happened to me. I made myself sick.—Junior 10

When consultants get sick for a longer period like junior 10, it often means a burnout. Not only junior 10 reports illness when reflecting on the leadership style illustrated in the cartoon, also managers recognize this is happening increasingly:

> What I do see, is the age at which people come down with long-term illness is rapidly declining. I have an increasing number of people under 30 coming to me with such symptoms.—Manager 3

Next to burnout, there are other health effects indicated like lowered wellbeing and lowered motivation, both impacting performances. Manager 5 illustrates what happens when leadership becomes over demanding, and how consultants lose motivation:

> If you are not handling them [the stressors of consulting] well, you see that in your performance. Then you don't even like working here, and you couldn't care less about performance.—Manager 5.

What makes the problem bigger is that managers do not notice overload problems often, and juniors do not share:

> Often juniors are ashamed, like, I am so young, why does it happen to me? As a manager you often discover it [overload struggles] later than their direct environment, and that it does not go well.—Manager 3.
>
> I know myself. I sure have my issues here. But I would never go with those to my boss […] opening up could be seen as a loss of face.—Junior 4.

Ultimately consultants make choices. Both managers and juniors report that management requiring 80 h of work and high levels of commitment is not sustainable in the end. It only works over a shorter period of time:

> In the moment you are like 'Okay, we have to get through this'. But you know it's not sustainable. You can't let juniors work that many hours for several weeks on projects. You know that they will leave after a year or so. It's not sustainable.—Manager 12.

Further elaborations thus go into health effects like burnout, the competitive work culture, the problem of not feeling you can share your struggles, the problem of losing motivation, and people drawing conclusions like leaving consulting. These associations all go beyond the direct content of the cartoon. They are invited, or triggered.

While the first interpretative answers focus more on what the cartoon tells, and to what extent it illustrates consultants work practice and experienced leadership, that is only the beginning of the conversation. During the interviews consultants do not only confirm, add nuance, or explain how the cartoon covers their daily reality. They also go deeper and illustrate effects for their health and wellbeing, not directly covered in the cartoon, but clearly related to the experience of the respondents. They also discuss what comes before the cartoon by detailing the work culture, the client demands, and the high standards.

3.3.3 Jokes-Based Interviews and Their Contribution to Ethical Research Questions

When relating the leadership cartoon to interviewee experiences, leadership in the context of consulting is assessed as unethical due to overly high demands. While the cartoon suggests ironically only positive wellbeing consequences, when asking consultants, they instead mention negative health and wellbeing consequences. The cartoon thus invites critical consequentialist reflections. For respondents the irony is not difficult to see. The cartoon sparks the discussion, invites various responses, and fosters exploration.

Responses also share deontological reflections. Working 80 h does not fit within the limits of labour law. That judgement is invited by the cartoon. The reader needs to know about labour law to be able to see this implied criticism. Labour law is designed with the intention to keep people healthy by keeping workhours reasonable. Interviewees discuss how staying within these normal limits has a low priority at consultancies. Other intentions like serving clients and making money are mentioned as the more central management priorities.

The management cartoon also inspires reflection on virtues. The presented over demanding manager is no virtuous leader. Compassion and being considerate are missing qualities in the managerial character depicted. The interview quotes confirm this managerial attitude with its focus on outputs and client satisfaction, more than on employee wellbeing. It is illustrative that the boss in the cartoon does not understand the complaints. This triggers all kinds of associations, memories of similar experiences, and evaluations of the work situation.

Starting the conversation with reflecting on carefully selected jokes invites deep conversations in the domains of business ethics, covering various grounds. Most ethical judgements in the cartoon are somewhat implicit or ironical, and need interpretation. That is what a reader needs to do when reflecting on the realities illustrated in the cartoon, and this is what happens in the conversation between interviewee and interviewer. The process of interpretation and making the ethical criticism explicit, entails much more than repeating what the cartoon tells. Interpretation means activating the implied norms and visualizing the consequences. When respondents interpret the cartoon in interviews, we see descriptive confirmation of the 80 h workweeks, partly also nuancing accounts, and explanations are given, but overall, there is a shared assessment that work pressures are too high too often.

Important for the method is the process of association towards the wider realities connected to the situation addressed in the cartoon: the stress, examples of lowered wellbeing, burnout, and consultants leaving as results of the leadership and performance culture experienced. Such observations receive a negative moral assessment from most of the interviewees. Explorative findings based on the jokes-based interview method supported a contribution to the literature on consulting ethics by shifting attention to the manager–consultant relationship, instead of only focussing on the client-consultant relation. Based on the explorative jokes-based interview method many more empirical and theoretical contributions can be expected in the field of business ethics, by answering open research questions like *how* business actors experience particular ethical transgressions addressed in jokes, or *how* they act on them.

3.4 Possibilities and Limitations of Jokes-Based Interviews

3.4.1 Critical Cartoons Stimulate Reflections on Business Ethical Transgressions

Starting open interviews by showing a cartoon offered a strong statement to start the conversation. The cartoon was initially confirmed or denied, but such responses were only the beginning. What happened next was that the cartoon was nuanced, which better fits an open interview approach, as cartoons and jokes mostly somewhat exaggerate or distort reality. Secondly, when a cartoon was sufficiently spot on, as with the cartoon indicating 80 h workweeks, it also triggered memories and released energy to talk about related issues. These could be causes and effects of the illustrated situation, but also moral leadership responses not indicated in the cartoon. Managers often recognized the problem and told how they acted on the situation (see Bouwmeester & Kok, 2018). To get such associative responses, the interviewer has to encourage the interviewee to go on and elaborate more by asking open follow-up questions related to the given answers: how did you do it, when, what happened next, who were involved and how, etc.

How to use cartoons as a trigger and starting point? Cartoons are very condensed in how they communicate, and thus leave a lot of the message implicit. They can be a starting point for further exploration in follow-up questions like: how does it happen in your work context, what did it mean to you when it happened, etc. The cartoons are a powerful icebreaker to start an exchange, but they need a follow-up conversation. Discussing ethical transgression in work life will usually cross the line of social desirability, and then denial is a common coping strategy. Cartoons can help to get beyond this denial by their humour, and they stimulate topical associations that create opportunities for further exploration in such areas. When the conversation has started, open interview techniques can follow, including having a topic list, preparing some questions you could ask, etc. (cf. Hermanowicz, 2002; Legard et al., 2003; Schein, 2006, Chap. 5). Another way to move on is to ask for related relevant workplace jokes the respondent knows of, and would like to share.

How to move to the respondents' experiences? In case of confirmation, nuancing or association, it is important to relate the cartoons' critical messages to experienced unethical behaviour in the interviewees own work context. The cartoon is an invitation to talk about work experiences that could illustrate the cartoon and vice versa. While we found that all transgressions in the ethics top ten could be illustrated by jokes, the reverse is true as well. Good jokes can be illustrated with experiences. That is due to the normality condition of humour (Veatch, 1998). The normality condition therefore explains why funny cartoons are a perfect starting point for a conversation on the addressed topics. For an interview study, these shared experiences count. They give the good quotes for analysis. Associations sparked by the cartoon were often critical, but have also addressed moral leadership responses that were aiming at preventing negative health effects, or illustrated what the organisation has done to prevent the addressed issues. The associative process demonstrated in the interviews can be assessed as very open and explorative.

How to select the joke that works best in an interview? Because cartoons work with visual expression and limited text, they can transfer their message quite fast. Therefore, cartoons can be used very well in an interview setting, and probably better so than text jokes. Still, the topical match is important for selection. In addition, the cartoon helps breaking through defences of social desirability, by its humorous touch. However, a cartoon is only the beginning, as everything needs to be told and illustrated by the interviewee. In the end only little is said in a cartoon, and what is said is overly general, provocative, sometimes ironical, partly fictional etc. As a genre, a cartoon needs interpretation similar to a metaphor. It makes the match between the interviewees' experiences and the cartoon's content of great importance. If there is not much of a link, as with the strip joint joke, little or no stories will be triggered. To prevent a wrong selection, a test interview might help, and some try outs related to how the jokes work on people that could be your interviewees. Next to the good match, some variation between jokes is important, to cover as much perspectives as possible. In the end the selection should not be too big, as there should be enough time for interpretation, association, elaboration and discussing interviewees own related experiences. While three jokes is towards the lower end, ten might be a lot. Then it would be good to let the interviewee focus on three to five, out of these ten.

How do I report the research method? The next steps of open coding, axial coding and further analysis are no different from other in-depth open interview approaches. Still, it is important to describe the whole method in steps from the start and till analysis as asked for in Gioia et al. (2013) and Suddaby (2006). Reviewers expect

3.4.2 Method Limitation of Jokes-Based Interviews

A first limitation to consider is that jokes could be leading, and preselect answers like leading question do (cf. Alvesson, 2003). There is also a risk due to the stereotyping effect jokes can have. However, this has not been our experience. This might be due the fact that if there is a leading or stereotyping element in jokes or cartoons such as with the over demanding leaders, it is so provocative and so part of the genre, that it does not take you by surprise. Secondly, it is not the interviewer who makes the joke, or is suggesting the stereotype. It is a public joke that is shared. In addition, interviewees are in no way expected to agree with the joke. In contrast, it is very interesting for a researcher to see how some jokes do not resonate, or less well. Our strip joint joke might illustrate this, as most interviewees did not recognize the suggested experience of shame. Their hard work or the pressuring management is not something they would hide for family. With other types of dirty work hiding might happen, but consultants were not ashamed to share these aspects of their work.

Similar to the limitations addressed in chapter two, jokes, memes or cartoons entail humour bias, meaning that not all forms of ethical transgression have fun potential. Only the mild offense of ethical norms or moral expectations can be appreciated as funny (McGraw & Warren, 2010; Veatch, 1998). In addition, such benign norm violations focus on the negative only, not the positive. That is a limitation as well. When selecting jokes, the interviewer also needs to be aware of the fact that the more serious issues may not be addressed in jokes and cartoons. This limitation makes them the perfect start for an interview, but probably not a sufficient source of knowledge on all potential ethical issues. Still, to start explorations with the lighter issues is good practice, as the personal risks and social desirability bias related to the bigger issues will only increase, and they are not the best topics to open an interview with.

In addition, jokes are condensed and abstract. They do not go into rich description. They mostly focus on key aspects and some funny details. The illustrations given by interviewees based on their experiences need follow-up questioning to get into the rich descriptions. Therefore, cartoons or small text jokes can best be used as a starting point for triggering stories, and to subsequently explore these cases further. I have observed how respondents could not mention sensitive issues when first asking them a question in words only. However, when following up with looking at some cartoons and memes, giving space for interpretation, and subsequently asking for related experiences, then relevant memories were triggered, and stories could be told that were initially blocked.

3.4.3 Reviewer Perspectives on Jokes-Based Interviews and Possible Responses

The jokes-based interview method starts with giving respondents opportunity to look at cartoons or text jokes, interpret them, and then relate such interpretations to their own experiences. The method did not get much push back in the publication on moral or dirty leadership (Bouwmeester & Kok, 2018) in *International Journal of Environmental Research and Public Health* (IJERPH). Before we first got a rejection from another journal. The reason was that our contributions were partly contradicting results of earlier dirty work studies that only reported normalization responses. Also the connection with moral leadership studies to explain the other type of responses was not seen as appropriate or helpful, as earlier dirty work theories were considered the better point of reference. Therefore we had to find another place to publish.

The first reviewer of the IJERPH article asked us to make the coding process more transparent by adding an overview of code families with parent and child codes. The second reviewer asked for more information about the respondents, which we both did. Overall, the reviewers liked the method and could relate to the results and its implications for occupational health. That results were in line with their theoretical expectations must have made it easier to accept the new method. When reviewers see novel, somewhat provocative results based on a novel method, they may be more inclined to doubt the results.

When using the jokes-based interview method, a central concern in cases of rejection has been that using cartoons, memes or text jokes was expected to be leading. This has not been our experience. To mitigate this concern, I have shown how our interviewees came to their interpretations (cf. Alvesson, 2003) and how their stories clearly moved beyond the content of the jokes, demonstrating that jokes are only a starting point and trigger for the conversation. Jokes very much support doing open in-depth interviews. To further prevent a leading influence, it is good to emphasize during interviews that the jokes represent a public critique, independent of the researchers' judgement. Therefore, use a cartoon as the starting point for reflection, ask open follow-up questions related to the first responses, ask for illustrations, own experiences, and take it from there. The purpose is that interviewees move to their own narratives, stories, and descriptions of the events they have experienced.

In the jokes-based interview study of Bouwmeester et al. (2022) reviewers asked stronger motivations for using the new method, and mentioned Zaltman's metaphor elicitation technique. Zaltman (1996, 1997) gives respondents complete say in what images they would like to talk about, as being illustrative of a brand. While the search of illustrative jokes is quite laborious and not something you could ask from an interviewee, we could give respondents more jokes and let them select which ones feel most relevant to them. Zaltman has also mentioned that participants sometimes looked for images they could not find. Then he invited respondents to tell what pictures they were looking for, and what these images could have told. In the same way we could ask what moral critique was not well covered in the jokes, or how cartoons could be adapted to criticize better. We did not do so, but these are interesting possibilities to further develop the method.

Jokes only give the slightest bit of structure, much less than traditional semi structured interviews based on a topic list (cf. Hermanowicz, 2002; Legard et al., 2003). Still, due to the thematic focus given by the selected jokes, the jokes-based interview method is somewhat semi structured. Given its open character it works very well for explorative research questions and in nascent fields of research. While the method is already to the open side, it will be even more so if interviewees can select from a wider set of jokes. The method helps interviewees to open up if there is social desirability bias, such as when talking about ethical transgressions in business. Until today the dominant source of case knowledge in business ethics is what journalists report, which is a very clear indication that business ethics is very nascent in its empirical research of ethics cases (Edmondson & McManus, 2007). While journalists cover very severe cases mostly, business jokes invite to study the more common, mid-range transgressions we still know little about.

Acknowledgements This chapter is based on a research method as used in Bouwmeester and Kok (2018), a study published in *International Journal of Environmental Research and Public Health*.

References

Allen, J., & Davis, D. (1993). Assessing some determinant effects of ethical consulting behavior: The case of personal and professional values. *Journal of Business Ethics, 12*(6), 449–458.

Alvesson, M. (2003). Beyond neopositivists, romantics, and localists: A reflexive approach to interviews in organizational research. *Academy of Management Review, 28*(1), 13–33.

Alvesson, M., & Robertson, M. (2006). The best and the brightest: The construction, significance and effects of elite identities in consulting firms. *Organization, 13*(2), 195–224.

Ashforth, B. E., Kreiner, G. E., Clark, M. A., & Fugate, M. (2007). Normalizing dirty work: Managerial tactics for countering occupational taint. *Academy of Management Journal, 50*(1), 149–174.

Bouwmeester, O., Atkinson, R., Noury, L., & Ruotsalainen, R. (2021). Work-life balance policies in high performance organisations: A comparative interview study with millennials in Dutch consultancies. *German Journal of Human Resource Management: Zeitschrift Für Personalforschung, 35*(1), 6–32.

Bouwmeester, O., & Kok, T. E. (2018). Moral or dirty leadership: A qualitative study on how juniors are managed in dutch consultancies. *International Journal of Environmental Research and Public Health, 15*(11), 2506.

Bouwmeester, O., Versteeg, B., van Bommel, K., & Sturdy, A. (2022). Accentuating dirty work: Coping with psychological taint in elite management consulting. *German Journal of Human Resource Management, 36*(4), 411–439. https://doi.org/10.1177/23970022211055480

Edmondson, A. C., & McManus, S. E. (2007). Methodological fit in management field research. *Academy of Management Review, 32*(4), 1246–1264.

Gill, M. J. (2015). Elite identity and status anxiety: An interpretative phenomenological analysis of management consultants. *Organization, 22*(3), 306–325.

Hermanowicz, J. C. (2002). The Great Interview: 25 Strategies for Studying People in Bed. *Qualitative Sociology, 25*(4) 479–499. https://doi.org/10.1023/A:1021062932081.

Kihn, M. (2012). *House of lies: How management consultants steel your watch and then tell you the time*. Business Plus.
Krehmeyer, D., & Freeman, R. E. (2012). Consulting and ethics. In T. Clark & M. Kipping (Eds.), *The Oxford handbook of management consulting* (pp. 487–498). Oxford University Press.
Legard, R., Keegan, J., & Ward, K. (2003). In-depth interviews. In J. Ritchie & J. Lewis (Eds.), Qualitative research practice: *A guide for social science students and researchers* (Vol. 6, pp. 138-169). Sage.
McGraw, A. P., & Warren, C. (2010). Benign violations: Making immoral behavior funny. *Psychological Science, 21*(8), 1141–1149.
Meriläinen, S., Tienari, J., Thomas, R., & Davies, A. (2004). Management consultant talk: A cross-cultural comparison of normalizing discourse and resistance. *Organization, 11*(4), 539–564.
Mühlhaus, J., & Bouwmeester, O. (2016). The paradoxical effect of self-categorization on work stress in a high-status occupation: Insights from management consulting. *Human Relations, 69*(9), 1823–1852.
Noury, L., Gand, S., & Sardas, J.-C. (2017). Tackling the work-life balance challenge in professional service firms: The impact of projects, organizing, and service characteristics. *Journal of Professions and Organization*.
O'Mahoney, J. (2007). Disrupting identity: Trust and angst in management consulting. In S. C. Bolton & M. Houlihan (Eds.), *Searching for the H in human resource management: Theory, practice and workplace contexts* (pp. 281–302). Palgrave Macmillan.
O'Mahoney, J. (2011). Advisory anxieties: Ethical individualisation in the UK consulting industry. *Journal of Business Ethics, 104*(1), 101–113.
Poulfelt, F. (1997). Ethics for management consultants. *Business Ethics: A European Review, 6*(2), 65–70.
Redekop, B. W., & Heath, B. L. (2007). A brief examination of the nature, contexts, and causes of unethical consultant behaviors. *Journal of Practical Consulting, 1*(2), 40–50.
Rivera, L. A. (2016). *Pedigree: How elite students get elite jobs*. Princeton University Press.
Skagert, K., Dellve, L., Eklöf, M., Pousette, A., & Ahlborg, G. (2008). Leaders' strategies for dealing with own and their subordinates' stress in public human service organisations. *Applied Ergonomics, 39*(6), 803–811.
Vahl, R. (2013). Hard werken en gezond leven. *Gezond Ondernemen, 6*(2), 6–11.
Veatch, T. C. (1998). A theory of humor. *Humor-International Journal of Humor Research, 11*(2), 161–216.
Zaltman, G. (1996). Metaphorically speaking. *Marketing Research, 8*(2), 13–20.
Zaltman, G. (1997). Rethinking market research: Putting people back in. *Journal of Marketing Research, 34*(4), 424–437.

Open Access This chapter is licensed under the terms of the Creative Commons Attribution 4.0 International License (http://creativecommons.org/licenses/by/4.0/), which permits use, sharing, adaptation, distribution and reproduction in any medium or format, as long as you give appropriate credit to the original author(s) and the source, provide a link to the Creative Commons license and indicate if changes were made.

The images or other third party material in this chapter are included in the chapter's Creative Commons license, unless indicated otherwise in a credit line to the material. If material is not included in the chapter's Creative Commons license and your intended use is not permitted by statutory regulation or exceeds the permitted use, you will need to obtain permission directly from the copyright holder.

Chapter 4
Jokes-Based Survey Questions on Expert Virtues

4.1 Introduction to a Jokes-Based Survey Method

One of the main criticisms on consultants is their lack of expertise. Still, consultants are hired for their expertise, which appears paradoxical. When consultant expertise is lacking, the consequences for clients can be severe. In newspapers, bankruptcies have been related to the flawed, utopian or one-sided advice of consultants, absence of proper evidence, lacking guidelines for execution and recommendations that signal wishful thinking. The problem is acknowledged by consultants who list "being qualified" in their codes of conduct as first key value and important condition for their work. Being qualified is a virtue they identify with. However, as they often cannot sufficiently keep up with these standards, several jokes have picked up on the expertise issue.

When it comes to an assessment of consultant expertise, opinions may differ. For one group consultant expertise can be fine, while another group may be less convinced. This chapter starts here and seeks to find out *how a survey method using cartoon-based rating questions on consultant expertise can provide insights in stakeholder opinions.* Results are compared to those found with traditional statement-based rating questions on the same topic. Stakeholder opinions studied are those of clients, their employees, consultants themselves, academics studying consultants, and outsiders who are only informed by public sources. Each group has to rate traditional statements, and statements expressed in cartoons that criticize consultant expertise.

For philosophers and social scientists, it is relevant to study stakeholder opinions and their interests related to ethical issues, in this case lacking expertise. As the stakeholder configuration is quite complex for consultants with their own clients, client employees, the clients of clients etc., a method to study different perceptions of stakeholder groups regarding ethical issues helps to better understand for whom value is created or destroyed as suggested by Freeman (2010) and Krehmeyer and Freeman (2012). As with the jokes-based interview approach, the jokes-based survey method may help to get better access to the empirical material scholars in ethics need for

© The Author(s) 2023
O. Bouwmeester, *Business Ethics and Critical Consultant Jokes*,
SpringerBriefs in Ethics, https://doi.org/10.1007/978-3-031-10201-1_4

their ethics reflections, and the empirical material will be of better quality, than when only relying on journalistic accounts, traditional methods, or thought experiments.

The next sections will first review management literature on the paradox related to consultant expertise, second the design of our jokes-based survey method will be presented including some key outcomes this method has generated, and the chapter concludes with discussing possibilities and limitations of the jokes-based survey method for research in business ethics, including possible reviewer concerns.

4.2 The Issue—Opinions on Consultants' Lack of Expertise

Including cartoon-based survey questions to study opinions on professional ethics is a new mixed-method approach, here applied to the issue of consultant expertise and its flaws. Unlike law or medicine, consultancy as a profession does not have entry requirements or a generally accepted, common body of knowledge (Exton, 1982; Glückler & Armbrüster, 2003). This can create an awkward situation where few differences exist between the expertise of consultants and the knowledge of their clients. Exton (1982, p. 212) argues: "One might well expect that those whose profession it is to counsel others should possess some knowledge not common to those counselled". Having sufficient expertise is therefore a key value in consultants' codes of conduct but also a common critique.

Still, expertise is reported to be one of the key reasons for hiring consultants (Poulfelt & Payne, 1994; Wood, 2002). Consultants but also several researchers, therefore, emphasize their skilled and qualified nature (Greiner & Metzger, 1983; Kubr, 2002). Schein (1990) and Saxton (1995) describe consultants' expert role as their most common role. Expert consultants intend to provide "helpful information relevant to the client's problem" (Saxton, 1995, p. 59). This infers an image of consultants as aiding clients who lack the expertise to arrive at the desired solutions on their own (Sturdy et al., 2009, p. 247). Given this importance, lack of expertise may imply huge consequences for clients, like letting them decide for a wrong alternative, or reorganise at the cost of too many employees.

Therefore, lack of necessary expertise does figure prominently in the list of common vices in consulting (see Chap. 2, Table 2.2), and prevention is therefore highly prominent in consultants' codes of conduct. The kind of problem addressed in the literature is that "consultancy means the absence of deeper knowledge, shallowness partly associated with fashions and fads as well as overpayment and an almost immoral attitude" (Alvesson & Johansson, 2002, p. 229). Related critiques point at the ambiguous and vague results consultants produce (Clark, 1995; Mitchell, 1994; Sturdy, 1997); the overly frequent use of standardized models including reusing old or repackaged ideas (Redekop & Heath, 2007; Sturdy, 2009; Whittle, 2006), and lack of industry knowledge (Sturdy, 2009; Sturdy et al., 2008). Critics also suggest consultants cover up through the use of jargon, storytelling, glossy brochures, slick PowerPoint presentations, and expensive suits (Alvesson & Johansson, 2002; Ashford, 1998; Clark & Salaman, 1998; Pinault, 2000; Whittle, 2006).

It is not unusual for professions to be both highly respected and widely criticized at the same time. Doctors, lawyers and politicians—like consultants—continue to be the butt of many critical jokes and the target of satire. Galanter (2005, p. 19), in his study about lawyer jokes, suggests that critical jokes "reveal that the qualities and actions for which the experts are despised are closely related to the things for which they are esteemed".

The paradoxical findings pose the question how different stakeholders feel about consultant expertise: are clients more critical than consultants themselves? What is the view of academics that study consultants and how do employees experience the expertise of consultants? The different groups may have different opinions. Moreover, such ambiguities might be difficult to capture with direct, unambiguous survey questions only. For that reason, we decided to include cartoons on consultant expertise in our study design, to allow for more ambiguous understandings of consultant expertise, and to better introduce the topic with its implied paradoxes.

The next section discusses a mixed-method survey approach that links stakeholder opinions to two cartoons criticizing consultants' lack of expertise, as applied in Bouwmeester and Stiekema (2015). By triggering respondents' memories and experiences in a different way by asking questions about critical expertise cartoons, respondents might also be more willing to answer the set of traditional questions on consultant expertise. While the method is applied to stakeholder opinions on one particular professional vice, this only is an example case. The method can be used to study stakeholder opinions on any professional vice that has been joked about, and where there might be some controversy.

4.3 Application—Using Expertise Cartoons to Study Opinions

4.3.1 Jokes-Based Survey Method: Rating Cartoons Next to Traditional Statements

For this quantitative study, stakeholders could rate critical cartoons next to traditional statements about consultant expertise. That makes this a mixed-method study that combines rating questions related to cartoons with more traditional, literal rating questions. The method assumes respondents have the interpretive abilities to understand cartoons as Doherty (2011) argues. Likewise, Sturdy et al. (2008) and Bouwmeester (2013) consider humorous discourse an attractive source to study a profession because people only laugh about things they recognize, feel or care about (Cohen, 1999; Veatch, 1998). Still, humorous representation is somewhat distorted, exaggerated, sometimes ironical, and thus in need of adequate interpretation. To check if we can assume valid interpretation, traditional survey questions next to cartoon-based questions help to see if interpretations are consistent across methods, and within respondent groups.

Stakeholder groups are defined as "groups who can affect or are affected by a corporation" (Freeman, 2010, p. 1). In the Bouwmeester and Stiekema (2015) study, we report opinions of five groups. For groups like clients of consultants or client employees, this affect is obvious, given that consultants directly influence them with their assignments. Academics can be affected by consultants as well when being competitors or rivals in doing contract research, and academics are also an interested party when consultants are the subject of their studies. We consider as outsiders those who base their image of consultants only on what they read in newspapers or hear about them from friends. Their knowledge is not based on their own direct experience, and their stakes must be relatively low. In contrast, consultants themselves as the fifth group are strongly affected by the work of other consultants in that they strive to maintain, change, but sometimes also undermine their shared professional image and reputation, especially when expertise is lacking.

We have asked these five different stakeholder groups the same questions on consultants' expert image: first questions related to two critical cartoons and then as follow-up traditional questions about consultants' expertise. We selected two cartoons found on the Internet, the first criticizing expertise as being superficial, the second criticizing consultants' empty rhetoric. The text of the two cartoons and a short description of the image can be found in Table 4.1.

Figure 4.1 shows the first cartoon to illustrate how the criticism is visualized that consultants lack expertise.

The underlying assumption in the cartoon is that it does not matter what you know as a consultant, it is enough to merely claim you are an expert. This corresponds to a criticized absence of deeper knowledge (e.g. Alvesson & Johansson, 2002; Sturdy, 1997).

Table 4.1 Cartoons used in survey on stakeholder views on consultant expertise

Cartoon images, texts and web addresses
Cartoon 1: showing a man behind a desk, talking over the phone to a potential client, saying: "I know nothing about the subject, but i'm happy to give you my expert opinion." Bill and Eric Teitelbaum (27/3/2007), series Bottomliners • Retrieved from: www.gocomics.com/bottomliners/2007/03/27 • Last accessed 30 April 2021
Cartoon 2: showing a dialogue between and Dogbert and Ratbert in three pictures: 1. Dogbert: Ratbert, I'm going back into the consulting business and I need you to be my engagement manager 2. Dogbert gives Ratbert a piece of paper with a list of words and continues: You'll seem very smart if you randomly combine the words on this list and make many references to "Wal-Mart." 3. At the client Ratbert uses the list saying: It's like "Wal-Mart." Migrate you value into the white spaces of the ecosystem. As a response he gets: Wow! That's one smart rat! Scott Adams (3/3/1997) • Retrieved from: www.dilbert.com/strip/1997-03-03 • Last accessed 30 April 2021
Both cartoons can also be found in Bouwmeester and Stiekema (2015, p. 2443): https://research.vu.nl/ws/portalfiles/portal/122529082/The_paradoxical_image.pdf

4.3 Application—Using Expertise Cartoons to Study Opinions

Fig. 4.1 Cartoon 1 illustrating lack of expertise. © 2007 Tribune Content Agency, LLC All rights reserved

The second cartoon reflects the criticism that consultants' rhetoric can be empty, by concealing lack of expertise behind buzzwords and storytelling. Dogbert's engagement manager (Ratbert) applies such techniques. He is the consultant who is responsible for managing the relation with the client. The rhetoric may impress clients, and trick them into believing consultants on the team have sufficient expertise (e.g. Alvesson & Johansson, 2002; Clark & Salaman, 1998).

Stakeholder groups were initially approached by spreading a link to the survey via LinkedIn groups aimed at consultants and managers, and via the authors' networks. Respondents were asked various questions in order to help identify their stakeholder group, before asking them to rate cartoons. This initial strategy sufficiently motivated most stakeholder groups to answer the questions, but academics where not reached well. Therefore, we added a second round of outreach with direct emails to academics known for their publications on consultants. This ensured sufficient group size. The final sample size consisted of 216 respondents (consultants 22%, clients 26%, client employees 19%, academics 17%, outsiders 16%). The survey was opened for response for one month.

Since this research compares multiple groups, we used one-way ANOVA tests combined with a post hoc Tukey–Kramer test to identify specific differences between groups. Subsequently, the results were controlled with a Games-Howell test due to the fact that sample sizes were unequal. When performing ANOVA tests, the data should ideally comply with two assumptions (Field, 2009). First is the assumption concerning the normality of the distribution. This research complies with this criterion due to the sample sizes used: "The central limit theorem shows that for sample sizes greater than 5 or 10 per group the means are approximately normally distributed regardless of the original distribution" (Norman, 2010, p. 628). Second, we assume homogeneity of variance, which was tested with a Levene test where significance levels higher than 0.05 indicate homogeneous data. While in some cases the data lacked such homogeneity, we still choose to conduct ANOVA tests because ANOVA remains a robust test for such unequal variances (Glass et al., 1972; Lix et al., 1996).

4.3.2 Survey Results: Cartoon-Based and Statement-Based Responses

To study stakeholders' opinions on consultants' expertise we asked respondents to assess the two cartoons discussed in the methods section. The respondents were first asked to consider how funny they thought the cartoons were by assigning them stars from 1 (not funny) to 5 (very funny).

Next, they were asked about the extent of truth portrayed by these cartoons, and finally whether or not they reflected their own perception of consultants. These responses were given on a five-point scale (strongly disagree, disagree, neither agree nor disagree, agree, strongly agree). Table 4.2 presents a summary of the results.

Table 4.2 illustrates that all stakeholder groups consider the cartoons funny. They give the two cartoons on average a rating of 3 stars or a bit more, and without significant differences between the groups. Groups somewhat agree with the statement that the cartoons have a kernel of truth (average value 3.2), and again without significant differences between groups.

When answering the question of whether respondents had similar perceptions of consultants' *image*, as indicated by the two cartoons, the group of client employees agreed significantly more (3.28 first cartoon and 3.45 s cartoon) than clients (2.64 and 2.73) and consultants (2.38 and 2.55). Opinions are not very strong, but clients and consultants tended to disagree with the image expressed by the cartoons while client employees agreed, suggesting that the humour displayed by the cartoons contained an element of bitterness for client employees. Academics and outsiders held an intermediate position with a rather neutral opinion.

Table 4.3 summarizes the responses gathered with traditional survey questions about consultants' expertise. The differences in reactions displayed between the five stakeholder groups are in line with responses to the cartoon questions summarized in Table 4.2.

4.3 Application—Using Expertise Cartoons to Study Opinions

Table 4.2 Stakeholder views on consultant expertise: cartoon-based questions

Questions	Statistical differences between 5 groups	
	ANOVA	Tukey-Kramer
Cartoon 1: Funniness Av. $\bar{X} = 3.25$ SD = 1.050	No group differences $F(4,211) = 1.630$, $p = 0.168 > 0.05$	None $p > 0.05$
Cartoon 2: Funniness Av. $\bar{X} = 3.00$ SD = 1.119	No group differences $F(4,211) = 1.957$, $p = 0.102 > 0.05$	None $p > 0.05$
Cartoon 1: Kernel of truth Av. $\bar{X} = 3.24$ SD = 1.029	No group differences $F(4,211) = 0.552$, $p = 0.716 > 0.05$	None $p > 0.05$
Cartoon 2: Kernel of truth Av. $\bar{X} = 3.21$ SD = 0.998	No group differences $F(4,211) = 1.859$, $p = 0.119 > 0.05$	None $p > 0.05$
Cartoon 1: Reflects the image of consultants Av. $\bar{X} = 2.82$ SD = 1.037	Yes $F(4,211) = 5.386$, $p = 0.000 < 0.001$	Between Client Employees (M = 3.28) and Clients (M = 2.64), $p < 0.05$ Between Client Employees (M = 3.28) and Consultants (M = 2.38), $p < 0.001$ Between Academics (M = 3.03) and Consultants (M = 2.38), $p < 0.05$
Cartoon 2: Reflects the image of consultants Av. $\bar{X} = 2.91$ SD = 1.046	Yes $F(4,211) = 5.040$, $p = 0.001 < 0.01$	Between Client Employees (M = 3.45) and Clients (M = 2.73), $p < 0.01$ Between Client Employees (M = 3.45) and Consultants (M = 2.55), $p < 0.001$

All stakeholder groups tend to agree that consultants are good at understanding a company's specific problems (average 3.58) and are able to structure complex situations (average 3.56). It can, therefore, be concluded that criticisms about consultants' expertise do not focus directly on their diagnostic and analytical abilities. All stakeholder groups grant them their skills in this respect.

Also the average perception about the relevance of consultant knowledge is moderately positive, however, there are significant differences displayed among groups. Client employees, academics and outsiders are rather neutral, seeing less relevance of consultant knowledge than consultants (average 3.60) and clients even more (average 3.80).

When asked about the superficiality of methods used by consultants, client employees (3.57) and academics (3.37) tend to agree. On the other hand, clients and consultants tend to disagree with values somewhat below 3. The same logic applied to questions regarding the claim that consultancy expertise is flawed: clients and consultants slightly disagree with this claim while client employees agree significantly more with this criticism (3.45).

Tables 4.2 and 4.3 both demonstrate that client employees are the most negative stakeholder group when it comes to consultants' expertise, not seeing much relevance of consultants' knowledge and criticizing the superficiality of their methods and

Table 4.3 Stakeholder opinions on consultant expertise: traditional questions

Statements	Statistical differences between 5 groups	
	ANOVA	Tukey-Kramer
Consultants are competent at structuring complex situations Av. $\overline{X} = 3.58$ $SD = 0.808$	No $F(4,211) = 1.672$, $p = 0.158 > 0.05$	None $p > 0.05$
Good at understanding the specific problem of a company Av. $\overline{X} = 3.56$ $SD = 0.822$	No $F(4,211) = 1.646$, $p = 0.164 > 0.05$	None $p > 0.05$
Consultants have much relevant knowledge Av. $\overline{X} = 3.46$ $SD = 0.806$	Yes $F(4,211) = 6.037$, $p = 0.000 < 0.001$	Between Clients (M = 3.80) and Outsiders (M = 3.34), $p < 0.05$ Between Clients (M = 3.80) and Academics (M = 3.24), $p < 0.01$ Between Clients (M = 3.80) and Client Employees (M = 3.12), $p < 0.001$ Between Consultants (M = 3.60) and Client Employees (M = 3.12), $p < 0.05$
Consultants apply superficial methods Av. $\overline{X} = 3.11$ $SD = 0.994$	Yes $F(4,211) = 5.610$, $p = 0.000 < 0.001$	Between Client Employees (M = 3.57) and Clients (M = 2.91), $p < 0.05$ Between Client Employees (M = 3.57) and Consultants (M = 2.72), $p < 0.001$ Between Academics (M = 3.37) and Consultants (M = 2.72), $p < 0.05$
Consultants have flawed expertise Av. $\overline{X} = 3.07$ $SD = 0.960$	Yes $F(4,211) = 4.089$, $p = 0.003 < 0.01$	Between Client Employees (M = 3.45) and Consultants (M = 2.83), $p < 0.05$ Between Client Employees (M = 3.45) and Clients (M = 2.80), $p < 0.01$

their flawed expertise. Clients and consultants had the most positive opinion on the relevance of consultants' knowledge, the value of their methods and the quality of their expertise, indicating an overall belief in consultants' competences, which explains there is a market for consultant services. Outsiders and academics stay close to the average in their judgements, not having a strong opinion on consultant expertise.

The results in this mixed-method design are consistent, no matter if the questions are asked in a traditional way, or based on an expertise cartoon. All groups agree on the relatively strong analytical and diagnostic abilities of consultants. This is a positive aspect that gets lost in critical cartoons. Cartoons in general might be less suitable to point at strengths. A the positive side, they add to the validity of the survey, when used as control questions, and they motivate respondents to complete the surveys. These benefits can be profited from in business ethics research with its social desirability issues but also in research on other topics that can invite a critical laugh, like fashion, tradition, culture, etc.

4.3.3 Jokes-Based Survey Method and Contributions to Ethical Research Questions

We found that respondents were very able to interpret implied messages of the selected cartoons, as results were consistent with answers on traditional rating questions. Therefore, we can also consider the cartoon-based questions valid. The two cartoons have a kernel of truth according to all groups and both cartoons receive a rating of three stars for funniness. That means the normality condition for humour was met, and sufficient respondents recognized the issue.

When asking if the cartoons also adequately reflect the expert *image* of consultants, the groups start disagreeing. The same kind of disagreement appears when asking about expertise based on traditional statements regarding the relevance of consultant knowledge, their superficial methods and their flawed expertise. Client employees agree more with the virtue ethical critiques, clients and consultants do laugh but also tend to disagreement.

As consultants and clients are rather positive about consultants' knowledge and expertise, they do not seem to observe negative ethical implications due to any lack of consultant expertise. Clients and consultants must feel that on average, all assignments considered, they can satisfy their own ethical standards and the standards as expressed in their codes of conduct regarding expertise and competence. No strong deontological critiques here. Client employees recognize consultants' incompetence the most. For them, implications of consultants' lack of expertise will be more negative on average.

The used cartoons do not indicate consequentialist critiques. Still, implied consequences of lack of expertise must fuel the more negative average opinion of client employees, who are always at the receiving end of what clients and consultants plan for them. Consequences of incompetence are mostly experienced by them, and may thus strongly influence their view of consultants' professional image.

With the jokes-based survey method, we could contribute to debates in business ethics related to consultants' expertise paradox. Usually, the client is pictured as victim of consultants in the literature, but it seems more an ally here. Client employees and maybe other stakeholders in the client system are the ones who suffer most from consultants' incompetence, and they pay the price. These realized contributions show the method's value as addition to the sparse research methods in business ethics. The method contributions are mainly descriptive, by quantifying and comparing differing opinions on consultants' expert virtues. The jokes-based survey method can thus examine research questions like *the extent* to which different stakeholders' perceptions of ethical transgressions are aligned on various dimensions.

4.4 Possibilities and Limitations of a Jokes-Based Survey Method

4.4.1 How to Make Use of Cartoon-Based Rating Questions in a Survey

We can conclude that cartoon-based questions in a survey related to unethical business behaviour give good results, just like traditional statement-based questions that respondents have to rate on a five-point Likert scale. Results are consistent across these different forms of questioning, and so for the different stakeholder groups. Cartoons visualize ethical transgression, and leave no doubt on the implied judgement. Still, the method requires proper cartoon selection, and careful selection of respondents, who should have the ability to interpret the cartoons well. Then, adding jokes-based question to a survey can have several advantages when studying business ethical transgressions.

How do I select cartoons? An important condition is that the researcher has sufficient context knowledge and is able to interpret the jokes well. Designing a survey depends very much on the researcher. The selected cartoons need to be sufficiently on topic and understandable by experts as well as respondents. To check this out, pretesting the survey is needed. As an alternative for cartoons short text jokes could be selected if they relate better to the topic under investigation, but cartoons usually have a stronger expression.

How do I select respondents? Respondent selection is as important, as they need to be able to interpret the jokes. Therefore, send the survey to places where you can assume respondents have the context knowledge that is needed to understand the cartoons. A lawyer better understands lawyer jokes, and a consultant better understands consultant jokes. The same applies to their stakeholders. Understanding business jokes is a bit more challenging than understanding literal questions on the same topic, due to aspects like fiction, irony, abstraction, exaggeration and distortion.

How can cartoons increase response rates? Response rates benefit from the humour touch in a survey when cartoons are included. It gives respondents a laugh, while filling in just another survey. If they know this up front as an introduction to the link, it can be used as motivation to open the form and fill it in. In addition, the completion rate may benefit as well, as seeing some cartoons during the survey works like a reward. It should not be overkill though, as the length of the survey can undermine these positive effects. Also a cartoon you do not understand, or that is off topic, will not work motivational. Still, because people are different in how they process information, adding cartoon-based questions is attractive. Some respondents will have a more visual mind, and may drop out earlier when they have to process text only.

How can cartoon-based questions in a survey increase validity? Cartoon-based questions can be used to address sensitive ethical topics, and topics that invite a laugh or show ambiguity. A good cartoon adds clarity to a rating question, by its visualizations. For instance, lack of expertise may sound vague. How little expertise would that be? When looking at the expertise cartoon (Fig. 4.1), it is stated that any expertise is missing related to the question the client asks. In consulting your expertise can always be better, you learn on the job, but such absence of expertise is not meant in the cartoon. It is a more extreme version, which is discussed as part of the ethics top ten under 'underperformance' as one of its consequences. By using the cartoon, it becomes very clear what kind of incompetence is meant. Complete lack of knowledge on the subject is no average situation, but still one that happens enough to be common. Indeed, to be perceived as funny, cartoons have to meet the normality condition of humour (Veatch, 1998). To further increase validity, we used a mixed-method design and asked literal question and the cartoon-based questions on the same topic. These two types of questions work as a control and enable you to triangulate findings.

How can cartoons reduce social desirability bias? Based on what happened during cartoon-based interviews, the use of humour and visuals can make the respondent more open, gives them better access to memories, and reduces some internal barriers about what can be said and what not. When this happens, also the answers on traditional questions may benefit from using a mixed method design. By using humour in the survey design, we can get closer to the respondents' views on professional vices.

4.4.2 Method Limitations of Jokes-Based Rating Questions in a Survey

A first limitation of using cartoons in a jokes-based survey is that there is little possibility to go beyond the cartoon. Rating questions as common in quantitative designs have a very closed way of asking. A respondent can agree or disagree in degrees, but can add nothing different, or cannot indicate agreement with a slightly modified version of the question or in this case the joke. While open or semistructured interview questions give more room to respondents, rating questions cannot explore the associations triggered by cartoons. Rating questions also very much depend on the available jokes and their topics and statements. Open questions could be added to surveys as a remedy, but good opportunities to further explore what respondents have in mind are absent. The interpretation of responses to such open questions is also difficult, due to lack of context knowledge that is relevant to the respondent, but unknown to the researcher, and lack of opportunity to ask follow-up questions. It is also difficult to see if the respondent gets the joke, and if there is interpretation bias. That makes the mixed method design important, as it allows for control.

Second, there is humour bias. Cartoons focus on the negative, the imperfect, the abnormal etc. While traditional rating questions in a survey can relate to all kinds of statements ranging from positive to negative, cartoon statements tend to be critical. That makes the use of cartoon-based rating questions limited. When cartoons relate to ethics or business ethics, the focus is mainly on transgressions, as having virtues or good intentions is less funny (except maybe in more criminal, streetwise environments). In addition, jokes make fun of not meeting moral expectations that happen somewhat regularly. While they need to be emotionally absurd, transgressions should also be sufficiently common, or somewhat normal (cf. Veatch, 1998). In addition, transgressions cannot be too painful or too bad, as then the fun factor disappears. That limits the range of topics cartoons can address.

A third limitation linked to the topic of ethical transgressions pertains to how visible unethical behaviour is. Visibility is a condition for making cartoons. It is impossible to show something as funny that cannot be visualized, even if the transgression is sufficiently common. What seems to be visible enough though is character, and behavioural consequences, but intentions, identification with values or principles is much more difficult to visualize. This might explain why cartoons with ethical criticism focus predominantly on vices and problematic consequences. Transgressions without visible consequences may stay hidden, or require other forms of humorous expression.

4.4.3 Reviewer Perspectives on Jokes-Based Surveys and Possible Responses

The method using cartoon-based survey questions has been applied in an article submitted to the section of non-traditional research in the journal *Management Decision*. Bouwmeester and Stiekema (2015) got accepted after two rounds of reviews. It was the first submission, so no other journals have reviewed the method.

Method concerns raised by the reviewers were about better explaining how the methodology was a *mixed*-method approach, and how it draws on an interpretive epistemology for the questions based on cartoons (Czarniawska, 1997). For the traditional survey questions, interpretation was also needed, but not more than normal in a survey, and so it needed no further explanation.

One reviewer commented on the method with a statement like: "I actually liked the methods—a bit simple, but clever enough to give the reader a reason to continue" and after the first revision: "I think the humour method is intriguing". Concerns related to our group comparisons, that gave very descriptive results initially. The main challenge was to tell a good theoretical story, and to find an angle to better frame the results. We responded by interpreting the results from a rhetorical point of view, by looking at audiences and their interests.

When applying the method to other vices than lack of expertise, or linked to other professions, the mixed-method survey design should be applicable as well. Critical cartoons that address the issue need to be available of course, and for a stakeholder comparison, some controversy is needed as well. Alternatively, opinions on values that change over time can be studied when criticisms in cartoons change, or when perceived funniness of cartoons decreases over time, due to what is or isn't a mild violation of norms anymore.

Acknowledgements This chapter is based on a research method used in Bouwmeester and Stiekema (2015), a study published in *Management Decision*.

References

Alvesson, M., & Johansson, A. (2002). Professionalism and politics in management consultancy work. In R. Fincham & T. Clark (Eds.), *Critical consulting: New perspectives on the management advice industry* (pp. 228–246). Blackwell.

Ashford, M. (1998). *Con Tricks: The shadowy world of management consultancy and how to make it work for you.* Simon & Schuster.

Bouwmeester, O. (2013). Consultant jokes about managing uncertainty: Coping through humor. *International Studies of Management & Organization, 43*(3), 41–57.

Bouwmeester, O., & Stiekema, J. (2015). The paradoxical image of consultant expertise: A rhetorical deconstruction. *Management Decision, 53*(10), 2433–2456.

Clark, T. (1995). *Managing consultants: Consultancy as the management of impressions.* Open University Press.

Clark, T., & Salaman, G. (1998). Creating the 'right' impression: Towards a dramaturgy of management consultancy. *Service Industries Journal, 18*(1), 18–38.

Cohen, T. (1999). *Jokes: Philosophical thoughts on joking matters.* University of Chicago Press.

Czarniawska, B. (1997). *A narrative approach to organization studies.* Sage Publications.

Doherty, E. M. (2011). Joking aside, insights to employee dignity in "Dilbert" cartoons: The value of comic art in understanding the employer—employee relationship. *Journal of Management Inquiry, 20*(3), 286–301.

Exton, W. (1982). Ethical and moral considerations and the principle of excellence in management consulting. *Journal of Business Ethics, 1*(3), 211–218.

Field, A. (2009). *Discovering statistics using SPSS.* Sage Publications.

Freeman, R. E. (2010). *Strategic management: A stakeholder approach.* Cambridge university press.

Galanter, M. (2005). *Lowering the bar: Lawyer jokes and legal culture.* University of Wisconsin Press.

Glass, G. V., Peckham, P. D., & Sanders, J. R. (1972). Consequences of failure to meet assumptions underlying the fixed effects analyses of variance and covariance. *Review of Educational Research, 42*(3), 237–288.

Glückler, J., & Armbrüster, T. (2003). Bridging uncertainty in management consulting: The mechanisms of trust and networked reputation. *Organization Studies, 24*(2), 269–297.

Greiner, L. E., & Metzger, R. O. (1983). *Consulting to management.* Prentice-Hall.

Krehmeyer, D., & Freeman, R. E. (2012). Consulting and ethics. *The Oxford handbook of management consulting* (pp. 487–498). Oxford University Press.

Kubr, M. (2002). *Management consulting: A guide to the profession.* International Labour Organization.

Lix, L. M., Keselman, J. C., & Keselman, H. J. (1996). Consequences of assumption violations revisited: A quantitative review of alternatives to the one-way analysis of variance F test. *Review of Educational Research, 66*(4), 579–619.

Mitchell, V.-W. (1994). Problems and risks in the purchasing of consultancy services. *Service Industries Journal, 14*(3), 315–339.

Norman, G. (2010). Likert scales, levels of measurement and the "laws" of statistics. *Advances in health sciences education, 15*(5), 625–632.

Pinault, L. (2000). *Consulting demons: Inside the unscrupulous world of global corporate consulting.* Wiley.

Poulfelt, F., & Payne, A. (1994). Management consultants: Client and consultant perspectives. *Scandinavian Journal of Management, 10*(4), 421–436.

Redekop, B. W., & Heath, B. L. (2007). A brief examination of the nature, contexts, and causes of unethical consultant behaviors. *Journal of Practical Consulting, 1*(2), 40–50.

Saxton, T. (1995). The impact of third parties on strategic decision making: Roles, timing and organizational outcomes. *Journal of Organizational Change Management, 8*(3), 47–62.

Schein, E. H. (1990). A general philosophy of helping: Process consultation. *Sloan Management Review, 31*(3), 57–64.

Sturdy, A. (2009). Popular critiques of consultancy and a politics of management learning? *Management Learning, 40*(4), 457.

Sturdy, A. (1997). The consultancy process: An insecure business? *Journal of Management Studies, 34*(3), 389–413.

Sturdy, A., Clark, T., Fincham, R., & Handley, K. (2008). Management consultancy and humor in action and context. In S. Fineman (Ed.), *The emotional organization: Passions and power* (pp. 134–150). Blackwell.

Sturdy, A., Werr, A., & Buono, A. F. (2009). The client in management consultancy research: Mapping the territory. *Scandinavian Journal of Management, 3*(25), 247–252.

Veatch, T. C. (1998). A theory of humor. *Humor-International Journal of Humor Research, 11*(2), 161–216.

Whittle, A. (2006). The paradoxical repertoires of management consultancy. *Journal of Organizational Change Management, 19*(4), 424–436.

Wood, P. (2002). Knowledge-intensive services and urban innovativeness. *Urban Studies, 39*(5–6), 993–1002.

Open Access This chapter is licensed under the terms of the Creative Commons Attribution 4.0 International License (http://creativecommons.org/licenses/by/4.0/), which permits use, sharing, adaptation, distribution and reproduction in any medium or format, as long as you give appropriate credit to the original author(s) and the source, provide a link to the Creative Commons license and indicate if changes were made.

The images or other third party material in this chapter are included in the chapter's Creative Commons license, unless indicated otherwise in a credit line to the material. If material is not included in the chapter's Creative Commons license and your intended use is not permitted by statutory regulation or exceeds the permitted use, you will need to obtain permission directly from the copyright holder.

Chapter 5
Content Analysis of Critical Business Jokes

5.1 Introduction to a Jokes-Based Method of Content Analysis

When clients hire consultants, they may feel uncertain about the future of their company, the way their company is managed or if business opportunities are sufficiently spotted and acted on. Consultants may feel uncertain due to high client expectations. The challenge for both parties will be to manage these uncertainties. At the same time uncertainly creates opportunities for taking shortcuts, forms of misuse and manipulation. When such practices enter the grey zone of acceptability, they become joking material.

In critical management literature the position of managers is often presented as dependent on consultants. Business jokes however, paint a more balanced picture. This chapter seeks to find out *how content analysis of business jokes can generate new and valid insights on ethical transgressions related to uncertainties in the consultant–client relation.* As critical business jokes focus on key aspects in need of critique, they individually do not provide much detail. However, content analysis of a larger set of business jokes generates more differentiated understandings of the ethical challenges linked to uncertainties in the consultant–client relation. Method implications of using business jokes as a data source for content analysis relate to the often fictional, sometimes ironic and also one-sided character of the data source.

The relevance of jokes-based content analysis for business ethics is substantial, as it is a rich data source for studying ethical malpractice. Accounts are not so extreme as showing very criminal behaviour usually, but it is still unethical in various ways. That gives scholars in ethics access to more empirical materials to reflect on in business ethics. The method is very close to what philosophers are used to, as text interpretation is key to their profession. Social scientist also have a tradition in content and discourse analysis, including the analysis of metaphors and analogies, so the method is probably not too much of a stretch for most scholars interested in ethics.

The next sections will review critical consultant literature first, to see what we know about uncertainties in the consultant–client relation. Next the method of applying content analysis to jokes will be explained together with some results and their contributions to the field. The chapter concludes with possibilities and limitations of jokes-based content analysis in business ethics, including a discussion of possible reviewer concerns.

5.2 The Issue—Using Consultant and Client Uncertainties

Content analysis of business jokes to study professional ethics is a new research method, here applied to the ethical issue of use and misuse of uncertainty in the consultant–client relation. Uncertainty can have a double manifestation in this context. It first applies to the recommendations a consultant can give, because these can be given with more or less certainty. Secondly, uncertainty in the consultant–client relation concerns the person, as illustrated by Alvesson and Johansson (2002, p. 238) and Sturdy (1997). It is the personal experience of uncertainty or insecurity both on the side of the client and on the side of the consultant. The two forms of uncertainty interact with each other: ambiguous knowledge or uncertainty about the future impact of recommendations can induce a personal feeling of uncertainty.

As our rationality is bounded and our knowledge limited, clients can feel uncertain, but still want to act. Consultants may therefore emphasize the possible benefits of their recommendations and prefer not to articulate uncertainties, to avoid that these uncertainties may paralyse a client (Bouwmeester, 2010, p. 218). Consultants take pride in helping a client to move from a state of "uncertainty to a state of harmony and security" (Alvesson & Johansson, 2002, p. 239). To further reduce client uncertainty, consultants invest in building a good reputation (Poulfelt, 1997). Glückler and Armbrüster (2003) explain with institutional arguments that there are no accepted professional standards, and no contracts that can guarantee the quality of the consultancy service. A good reputation then helps to overcome these uncertainties.

However, pretending self-confidence and downplaying uncertainties is a risky tactic. Angner (2006, p. 18) argues that consulting economists are often "overconfident". The quality of their advice would improve by stressing uncertainties, not by ignoring them. Stiglitz (1998, p. 39) argues likewise that economic policy advice could improve by explicit recognition of uncertainties, however: "too often, that has not been the case." Such overconfidence of consultants can be criticized on ethical grounds as being reckless, or as bluff.

Even though consultants may often aim at uncertainty reduction, there are also situations in which they do the opposite and intentionally share their uncertainties (Fincham, 1999; 2002b) or actively create uncertainty. Fincham (1999, p. 339) explains how consultants can increase their clients' sense of uncertainty by firmly addressing their problems, which is a well-known tactic to obtain better acceptance of solutions they propose. Furthermore, creating a sense of urgency is seen as an important early step during planned change (Kotter, 1995). Clegg et al. (2004) even compare consultants with parasites who destabilize an organisation and purposefully create chaos.

Feelings of certainty or uncertainty do not only belong to clients. Although consultants present themselves as confident, certain in their approach, and "in control", Sturdy (1997, p. 405) questions such self-confidence. He argues that consultants must also experience feelings of uncertainty caused by the pressure to resolve uncertainties for their clients. He follows Jackall (1988, p. 141) who points at the dialectic between consultant services and client anxiety. Field research by Skovgaard-Smith (2008, p. 110) also shows how clients can purposefully create consultant uncertainties, to limit their impact.

A last dynamic can be characterized as making use of existing uncertainties. Such tactics are hardly discussed in the literature. They create opportunity for business bluffing (Boussebaa, 2008; Carr, 1968). If clients do not possess sufficient relevant knowledge, this tactic can work convincing, but from an ethics perspective this behaviour can be questioned. Furusten (2009) mentions improvisation as alternative tactic to make use of uncertainty. While referring to jazz improvisation, he argues that consultants also change roles and adapt activities in response to unexpected situations.

To show how uncertainties in the consultant–client relation are used and misused, this chapter uses a new method of content analysis that is applied to critical business jokes on the topic. The same approach is used in Bouwmeester (2013). Below I will discuss this new method of content analysis in more detail.

5.3 Application—Analysing a Sample of Critical Business Jokes

5.3.1 *Method of Jokes-Based Content Analysis: Sampling and Open Coding*

The example study to demonstrate the new method of content analysis uses a hermeneutic approach to interpret critical business jokes. Authors or audiences of jokes are unknown and have to be implied in the reading. Interpretations are based on content analysis, as used in grounded theory and document analysis (Altheide, 1987). The coding process during the analysis follows a number of iterative steps (Corbin and Strauss, 1990), and are made explicit as required in qualitative methods (Gioia et al., 2013; Suddaby, 2006).

The search for business jokes used in this study was conducted on the Internet in 2012, using Google. The keywords used in the search were: "consultant," "consulting," "consultancy," "management consultant," "management consulting," and "management consultancy." Each of these words was combined with the word "joke" to find text jokes, and with the word "cartoon" to find cartoons. Moreover, each search was conducted twice, once with and once without quotation marks. The jokes collection is mainly Anglo-Saxon and includes various common topics consultants and their stakeholders criticize.

The collected jokes and cartoons were coded in AtlasTI. First, all jokes and cartoons from the sample were analysed for clues that relate to uncertainty, such as modal qualifiers, or activities that relate to uncertainty, such as bluffing. This resulted in a subsample of 31 cartoons and 13 jokes with a link to consultant or client uncertainty. Tentative codes were assigned to these 13 jokes and 31 cartoons indicating how they relate to uncertainty and how they are relevant to the subsample. Second, these codes were refined and consolidated. Third, the codes were organised in three code families (axial coding), illustrating uncertainty creation tactics, tactics that make use of uncertainty and uncertainty reduction tactics. Fourth, the tactics within each family were labelled as being client tactics, consultant tactics, or both.

Coding was done in several rounds to ensure that the codes were consistently applied to all jokes and cartoons, going back and forth between the four stages. Since the number of jokes and cartoons is relatively small, some codes are only grounded in one joke or cartoon. However, as the joke or cartoon adds a new perspective and a richer description to a code family, also one-time codes have been included for their unique contribution. All cartoons only illustrate one tactic. Some jokes illustrate more than one tactic, as the narrative is sometimes more complicated or detailed than in cartoons. The three code families, indicating the three types of tactics, are all well-grounded. Given the relatively small sample, more specific tactics with the three types may exist.

Table 5.1 presents an overview of the coded tactics and code families, and reports their groundedness in the cartoons (C) and jokes (J), meaning that there are many illustrations of the first tactic (consultants purposefully creating client uncertainty, problems, chaos): 6 in cartoons and 3 in jokes.

5.3.2 Results: Tactics Related to Client and Consultant Uncertainty

The study of uncertainty in the consultant-client-relation using jokes-based content analysis provides new insights in three areas. First there are tactics visible in the jokes that create uncertainty for the other side, second there are tactics that make use of uncertainties, and last there are tactics that aim at reducing uncertainty. Each of these tactics will be related to earlier discussions, to see what kind of detail or nuance is added to earlier knowledge based on this new method.

How clients and consultants create uncertainty The most dominant theme in uncertainty jokes is about consultants purposefully creating uncertainty by emphasizing client problems. Client uncertainty usually generates more work for consultants. One joke in this joke family has a classical form and discusses what is the oldest profession (physician, engineer or consultant):

5.3 Application—Analysing a Sample of Critical Business Jokes

Table 5.1 Tactics to create, use or reduce uncertainty found in jokes and cartoons

Codes	C	J	Sum
Tactics of uncertainty creation			
Purposefully create client uncertainty, problems, chaos (consultant)	6	3	9
Stress consultant's insecure position or lack of knowledge (client)	2	2	4
Create stakeholder uncertainty (consultant)	1	0	1
Tactics to use uncertainty			
Use client's uncertainty for claiming esoteric expertise (consultant)	5	0	5
Use client's uncertainty for nonsense advice or lies (consultant)	1	1	2
Choose strategically from conflicting expert opinions (client)	0	1	1
A consultant who hesitates is probably right (client)	0	1	1
Consultant tactics to reduce uncertainty			
Mitigate uncertainty by reframing, or redefining	3	2	5
Mitigate uncertainty by presenting obvious generalities	3	0	3
Mitigate uncertainty by being vague	3	0	3
Mitigate uncertainty by guessing	0	2	2
Reduce client uncertainty by suggesting positive thoughts	2	0	2
Reduce client uncertainty by selling a feeling of security	2	0	2
Reduce client uncertainty by reckless encouragement	1	0	1
Reduce own uncertainty by organising a solution or keeping distance	2	2	4
Reduce own uncertainty by referring to textbooks or spreadsheet	0	2	2

A physician, a civil engineer and a consultant were arguing about what was the oldest profession in the world.

The physician remarked, 'Well, in the Bible, it says that God created Eve from a rib taken out of Adam. This clearly required surgery, and so I can rightly claim that mine is the oldest profession in the world.'

The civil engineer interrupted, and said, 'But even earlier in the book of Genesis, it states that God created the order of the heavens and the earth from out of the chaos. This was the first and certainly the most spectacular application of civil engineering. Therefore, fair doctor, you are wrong: mine is the oldest profession in the world.'

The consultant leaned back in her chair, smiled, and then said confidently, 'Ah, but who do you think created the chaos?'

(http://www.workjoke.com/consultants-jokes.html#612).

Such subversive jokes about uncertainty creation by consultants are in line with the argument by Clegg et al. (2004), Kotter (1995) and Fincham (1999) who suggest that consultants stress uncertainties to prepare their clients for new solutions, a sense of urgency, and learning. Next to that, when change consultants help unlearning and relearning routines, organisations can feel chaotic. The jokes under this category indicate an immoral aspect, by stressing how much chaos consultants can create, instead of really helping or adding value as clients may expect. This way the jokes point at what Veatch (1998) considers emotional absurdity.

However, clients also create uncertainty for consultants. Two cartoons picture the consultant as being shot into a client organisation with a catapult or canon. In a cartoon from Andrew Toos made in 2004 clients are doing the shooting (https://www.cartoonstock.com/cartoon?searchID=CS247894). In a Dilbert cartoon from Scott Adams with Ratbert as consultant (www.dilbert.com/strip/1998-09-09), partners in the consultancy are doing the shooting. They can be seen as an internal client for employed consultants. As an observer you can imagine the fears and uncertainties consultants suffer in such an insecure position, making them the victims. Consultant insecurities caused by very demanding clients are addressed in the literature by Fincham (1999; 2002a, b), Jackall (1988), Skovgaard-Smith (2008) and Sturdy (1997), but the internal client relation has gotten less attention. Overall, what jokes and cartoons emphasize about the creation of uncertainty by consultants and clients can be related back to the literature on consultants quite well.

Use of uncertainty A next theme in the jokes is what consultants and clients do with client uncertainty, once it is there. Four cartoons stress the esoteric kind of knowledge consultants provide. Consultants are pictured as clergyman, or as mediums who receive messages from God or Satan. Similar to such cartoons you also find a joke with a consultant giving nonsense recommendations, when a client really does not know what to do. Below follows the second suggestion in a joke about a farmer who needs help to solve the problem of his dying chickens. The second recommendation is as ridiculous as the first one:

> [...] After a week the farmer came back to the consultant and said: 'My chickens continue to die. What shall I do?'
> 'Add strawberry juice to their drinking water, that will help for sure'.
> (http://nowthatisfunny.blogspot.com/2005/10/jokes-about-consultants.html).

Such characterizations of consultants resemble those of guru-consultants also pictured as "witch doctors" (Clark & Salaman, 1996; Micklethwait and Wooldridge, 1996) and "charlatans" (Bloomfield & Danieli, 1995, p. 39). Clients will suffer, being dependent on such consultants.

However, also consultants are portrayed as experiencing uncertainty and clients make use of this as well, as in the list joke: "Consulting revisited" two lines before the end:

> If you consult enough experts, you can confirm any opinion.
> (http://nowthatisfunny.blogspot.com/2005/10/jokes-about-consultants.html).

The joke "Consultant commandments" reflects an even more critical client position, where the client deconstructs how consultants present their views. It says on the fifth line:

> He who hesitates is probably right.
> (www.officehumorblog.com/index.php/2006/09/07/joke-240-consultant-commandments/)

These jokes criticize strategic uses of consultant uncertainty, and how clients make use of the frequent bluffing of consultants (cf. Boussebaa, 2008). Both parties seem

5.3 Application—Analysing a Sample of Critical Business Jokes

to engage in opportunistic use of each other's uncertainty, when interpreting the jokes carefully. Moral standards seem rather low on both sides, illustrating the argument of low ethical standards in business as made in Carr (1968).

Reducing uncertainty Tactics used by consultants to alleviate uncertainty are demonstrated in jokes and cartoon in most detail, resulting in the richest code family, based on the variation in tactics observed. A first subgroup of tactics illustrates how consultants influence clients' understanding of the question or task that creates uncertainty. A second group is directed at reducing client uncertainties, and a third group discusses how consultants usually manage their own feelings of uncertainty.

The techniques that target the task or question in the jokes are rhetorical, such as framing tactics. Consultants create certainty by their focus on the bigger picture while excluding 'exceptions' like Dogbert does in a Scott Adams cartoon from 2001:

> every company that used my six sigma program increased profits, except for the ones that were in industry downturns … or flat growth industries … or industries that only upturned a little bit.
>
> (https://dilbert.com/strip/2001-10-04).

Dogbert frames as exceptions what can be considered the rule. In the cartoons consultants also soften the perception of uncertainty by being vague and by talking in obvious generalities. Jokes also illustrate guessing approaches. Some of these rhetorical tactics of consultants to reduce uncertainty have been discussed in Berglund and Werr (2000, p. 652) and Bouwmeester (2010, p. 231), but the jokes and cartoons do add much detail here.

Second subgroup of tactics aiming at reducing uncertainty do not focus on the subject of investigation, but on the client. Five cartoons illustrate consultants providing reckless encouragement, selling positive thoughts and feelings of security or optimism, as in the John Morris cartoon from 1998 on consultants with the text: "Miss Smith, send in an optimist", while in the background a sales graph drops dramatically (www.cartoonstock.com/cartoonview.asp?catref=jmo0078). Alvesson and Johansson (2002) and also Sturdy (1997) have criticized this service of selling security and optimism without any substantial backing.

A third subgroup of tactics aims at reducing consultants' own uncertainties. A first tactic made fun of is how consultants organise the process, instead of being able to provide a solution directly:

> A priest, a rabbi and a consultant were traveling on an airplane. There was a crisis and it was clear that the plane was going to crash and they would all be killed. The priest began to pray and finger his rosary beads, the rabbi began to read the Torah and the consultant began to organise a committee on air traffic safety.
>
> (www.jokelabs.com/2007/10/987-priest-rabbi-and-consultant-in-airplane-that-going-to-crash.html).

The strategy to organise a search process for finding a solution is well known as means to cope with bounded rationality (March & Simon, 1993, p. 161), but the joke clearly identifies the limits of this approach when time is short. Another issue is that many consultants are young and inexperienced: "Top ten things a consultant shouldn't tell a client." On the sixth position: "Sure it'll work; I learned it in business school" and on the eighth: "Of course it's right; the spreadsheet says so." This is how consultants manage their inexperience according to the jokes. Especially consultants working for the big four, big three and big IT consultancies are known to be young. The average employee age in these companies is around 30 years, as they mostly hire fresh graduates (cf. Alvesson & Einola, 2018; Bouwmeester et al., 2021).

Reducing uncertainty can be beneficial when it prevents paralysis, but more often it will do what the jokes suggest, which is hiding and clouding an adequate understanding of risks, threats and real opportunities. Lack of knowledge comes with a price. You better know your margin of error when you start guessing. The consequences of following such shaky advice while believing it is sound, can be detrimental for clients.

5.3.3 Jokes-Based Content Analysis and Contributions to Ethical Research Questions

Content analysis of business jokes gives us new insights in the various ways consultants and their clients create, use and reduce uncertainty, and such tactics become unethical easily. First, creating uncertainty as a sales tactic is a form of manipulation, and creating uncertainty as a client to limit the impact of consultants is manipulation too. Such tactics will serve particular interests only. Second, using client uncertainties leads to bluffing. Usually this is not helping a client. Third, consultant tactics to reduce uncertainty like being vague, general or overly optimistic or positive mask a lack of vision. Also framing problems away, and using spreadsheets or textbooks to compensate for lack of expertise are common enough. Still, they all are far from virtuous and tend to self-interest, dishonesty, recklessness and uselessness.

As it is quite embarrassing to admit a lack of knowledge as a consultant, bluffing is an easy way out. Bluffing meets the normality condition of humour as it happens enough to be recognized by audiences. At the same time, such superficiality and incompetence is also funny because there is emotional absurdity, meaning the mild violation of standards that can be expected of a consultant. And it is as embarrassing for clients to admit they continuously hire such bluffing and deceiving consultants. The consequences of covering up uncertainty and the lack of competence are more often than not harming a client. Still, the first perspective to be critical here is virtue ethics.

The various tactics found based on content analysis of critical business jokes contribute to our knowledge of business ethical transgressions. The analysis shows a great variety of unethical business practices, some of them not discussed before. They also illustrate unethical behaviour on the sides of both clients and consultants, adding a more inclusive perspective than the mere focus on one side, as common in consulting literature, or studies on professions more general due to an overly narrow research focus.

Based on the contributions realized in this example study, more contributions to business ethics can be expected when using jokes-based content analysis in other contexts, or related to other professions. Jokes chose a moral perspective that cuts across the lines of disciplines or professions. As content analysis is an explorative research method, it will help to answer open research questions like *how* business actors behave unethical in certain areas or contexts.

5.4 Possibilities and Limitations of Jokes-Based Content Analysis

5.4.1 Larger Samples of Jokes Provide Richer Accounts of Ethical Norm Violation

For generating broader qualitative overviews of common ethical transgressions in a business field or profession, content analysis of business jokes is a very promising new method. Compared to academic literature on professional ethics of consultants, together the jokes and cartoons can add much detail. This applies for instance to tactics that reduce or use uncertainty, and the same applies to client strategies that make use of consultant uncertainty.

When ethical challenges receive sufficient attention in jokes, content analysis can offer many relevant insights. However, content analysis of jokes is different from analysing newspaper articles, consultant reports, annual reports or other forms of grey literature. Content analysis usually uses literal accounts as data, while jokes are like metaphors only partly true. They carry fictional elements, irony, abstraction, exaggeration, distortion, etc. To best distinguish fact from fiction and to get the most detailed insights, a large sample of jokes is needed. In addition, as interpretation of the jokes is fully dependent on the researchers, they need to have sufficient context knowledge related to the profession or industry of study. Outsiders will not get the jokes.

How do I create a big enough sample? The larger the sample of jokes about the chosen topic, the richer the analysis can be, as each different joke can provide a new angle. Between jokes there is much variation possible. Many business jokes qualify as insider jokes, so they can give away much detail. That makes them funny for business professionals and their colleagues, but less so for outsiders to a profession. My sample had 13 jokes and 31 cartoons, and I would consider that a small sample, that is towards the lower end. While it is good to make the sample as big as possible, it should remain closely linked to the ethical challenge you want to explore, to guarantee the quality of your sample. Also, when jokes are very similar and only slightly modified, better only take the best one of the two, as it can be seen as the same joke. If you feel the sample size is too small for content analysis, the jokes you have can still be used in jokes-based interviews, the method discussed in Chap. 3. Even with small samples, a tentative content analysis of some relevant jokes is always a very good starting point to get a feel for the ethical issues, next to a first review of relevant literature.

How can I distinguish fact from fiction, when doing open coding on jokes? A larger sample size helps a lot here: fiction shows great variation, while the more relevant factual elements will repeat themselves, showing a pattern. That is a form of data triangulation, comparing what the different jokes share about a particular ethical transgression. Triangulation with own experiences related to the field of study, with literature about the field, or with grey sources like research reports can help as well. The smaller the sample, the more these additional forms of triangulation are needed. However, compared to the other jokes-based methods, triangulation options are more limited for pure content analysis, as it cannot rely on what respondents tell when interpreting a joke.

How can I improve the coding and the required interpretation? It will improve the coding process to do this together with other field experts, and compare interpretations and discuss the codes. It improves intercoder reliability. Coding in several rounds also helps, and will improve consistency in the way transgressions are coded.

5.4.2 Method Limitations of Jokes-Based Content Analysis

Compared to the more common practice of illustrating ethical transgressions based on what journalists write, insights from business jokes shed light on common everyday transgressions, whereas journalists report the more extreme cases. The latter are newsworthy but provide little fun and usually qualify for anger as emotion. Cartoons are also published in newspapers to add opinion, but it is a balancing act often, to determine what can be made fun of, and what not. Public jokes focus on more frequent ethical transgressions in the grey zone of acceptability, such as the ones that figure in the top ten (see Table 2.2 in Chap. 2). Therefore content analysis of business jokes can be seen as a complementary source to journalistic case representations when studying business ethical transgressions.

The main methodological concerns when analysing business jokes to learn more about common ethical transgressions, relate to representation bias. To begin with, jokes are not considered to be truthful representations of reality, much like metaphors. Jokes are characterized by abstraction, distortion, exaggeration, stereotyping, irony and imaginative story telling approaches. They also tend to critique, and will ignore virtuous behaviour, or beneficial consequences. Still, they are dependent on some degree of truthfulness to be seen as funny, due to the normality condition of humour (Veatch, 1998). Seeing what is true and what is not, is up to those who interpret jokes or cartoons. As we recognize jokes as such, we know we have to do this. The larger the sample is, the more jokes we can compare on a topic, and the easier it is to distinguish fact from fiction. Content analysis of jokes is thus far more challenging, than content analysis of literal sources. Representation bias needs to be recognized and neutralized during the analysis by interpretation.

Second, there is humour bias. Not all topics, and also not all ethical transgressions are good material for joking. What is good material are the common, recognizable ethical transgressions that are kind of human, and understandable. What will not be represented in jokes are exceptional transgressions hardly anyone knows about, and very extreme transgressions no one can laugh about. The interpreter should be aware what kind of transgressions can be covered in jokes, and which ones are out of scope. Nevertheless, these insider jokes make a very good addition to the outsider accounts of journalists, that have a limited scope too.

Third, when doing content analysis, we need to consider interpretation bias. Interpretation is up to the researcher, but a researcher may have somewhat limited context knowledge: not completely up to date, not going back in time sufficiently, oriented on the Western world, a particular country, a business segment etc. No one is always able to understand every joke, or is familiar with the context and situation they refer to. To mitigate interpretation bias it helps to have sufficient knowledge about the professional field and a good sense of humour. Interpretation bias can also be reduced by comparing and discussing interpretations of multiple knowledgeable researchers. The same problem can happen on the side of reviewers, and wider audiences.

5.4.3 Reviewer Perspectives on Jokes-Based Content Analysis and Possible Responses

Content analysis of jokes is vulnerable to reviewer criticism. Reviews I have got after my initial success with a publication in *International Studies of Management and Organization* often criticized the data source. This has pushed me to develop the jokes-based interview and jokes-based survey methods in order to mitigate the given critiques. These other jokes-based methods create new kinds of data to rely on, and draw on broader interpretations than only those of the researcher. Still, I believe these criticisms indicated reviewer bias, as the bias in the source can be mitigated both by interpretation and data triangulation.

I wrote the article on uncertainties in the consultant–client relationship for a special issue on this topic, which created favourable conditions. All editors, and probably also the reviewers had context knowledge about the consultant profession, and were able to interpret the jokes and see their value. Still, they were also critical and wanted more explanations. After the first review I got as comment: "you need to provide more details on your method" which I did.

My hunch now is that reviewers and editors in the first project where consultancy scholars, while in the second attempt reviewers have been general management and ethics scholars, without the context knowledge needed to interpret the consultant jokes. They judged the jokes too much as if it was a literal data source, and considered it invalid, distorted, biased etc. As remedies they suggested more on the spot types of conversational analysis, where more context is provided and rich descriptions can be given. Such management and social science scholars identified more with qualitative traditions of anthropologists, and less with content analysis and interpretation as more common in the humanities.

My advice would be that when applying jokes-based content analysis as method in business ethics, articles can best be submitted to field journals linked to specific professions or sectors, to have reviewers and editors with sufficient context knowledge. Special issues on a relevant topic might also work, as editors and reviewers will then also be familiar with the literature and context relevant for interpreting the jokes. Not everyone is able to get a joke and reviewers, as representing one audience, are no exception.

Acknowledgements This chapter is based on a research method used in Bouwmeester (2013), a study published in *International Studies of Management and Organization*

References

Altheide, D. L. (1987). Reflections: Ethnographic content analysis. *Qualitative Sociology, 10*(1), 65–77.
Alvesson, M., & Einola, K. (2018). Excessive work regimes and functional stupidity. *German Journal of Human Resource Management, 32*(3–4), 283–296.
Alvesson, M., & Johansson, A. (2002). Professionalism and politics in management consultancy work. In R. Fincham & T. Clark (Eds.), *Critical consulting: New perspectives on the management advice industry* (pp. 228–246). Blackwel.
Angner, E. (2006). Economists as experts: Overconfidence in theory and practice. *Journal of Economic Methodology, 13*(1), 1–24.
Berglund, J., & Werr, A. (2000). The invincible character of management consulting rhetoric: How one blends incommensurates while keeping them apart. *Organization, 7*(4), 633–655.
Bloomfield, B. P., & Danieli, A. (1995). The role of management consultants in the development of information technology: The indissoluble nature of socio-political and technical skills. *Journal of Management Studies, 32*(1), 23–46.
Boussebaa, M. (2008). Book review: Are consultants simply bluffing? Sociologie du conseil en management by Michel Villette. *Organization, 15*(2), 298–300.
Bouwmeester, O. (2010). *Economic advice and rhetoric: Why do consultants perform better than academic advisers?* Edward Elgar.
Bouwmeester, O. (2013). Consultant jokes about managing uncertainty: Coping through humor. *International Studies of Management & Organization, 43*(3), 41–57.
Bouwmeester, O., Atkinson, R., Noury, L., & Ruotsalainen, R. (2021). Work-life balance policies in high performance organisations: A comparative interview study with millennials in Dutch consultancies. *German Journal of Human Resource Management, 35*(1), 6–32.
Carr, A. Z. (1968). Is business bluffing ethical. *Harvard Business Review, 46*(1), 143–153.
Clark, T., & Salaman, G. (1996). The management guru as organizational witchdoctor. *Organization, 3*(1), 85–107.
Clegg, S. R., Kornberger, M., & Rhodes, C. (2004). Noise, parasites and translation: Theory and practice in management consulting. *Management Learning, 35*(1), 31–44.
Corbin, J. M., & Strauss, A. (1990). Grounded theory research: Procedures, canons, and evaluative criteria. *Qualitative Sociology, 13*(1), 3–21.
Fincham, R. (1999). The consultant–client relationship: Critical perspectives on the management of organizational change. *Journal of Management Studies, 36*(3), 335–351.

References

Fincham, R. (2002a). The agent's agent: Power, knowledge, and uncertainty in management consultancy. *International Studies of Management & Organization, 32*(4), 67–86.

Fincham, R. (2002b). Charisma versus technique: Differentiating the expertise of management gurus and management consultants. In T. Clark & R. Fincham (Eds.), *Critical consulting: New perspectives on the management advice industry* (pp. 191–205). Wiley-Blackwell.

Furusten, S. (2009). Management consultants as improvising agents of stability. *Scandinavian Journal of Management, 25*(3), 264–274.

Gioia, D. A., Corley, K. G., & Hamilton, A. L. (2013). Seeking qualitative rigor in inductive research: Notes on the Gioia methodology. *Organizational research methods, 16*(1), 15–31.

Glückler, J., & Armbrüster, T. (2003). Bridging uncertainty in management consulting: The mechanisms of trust and networked reputation. *Organization Studies, 24*(2), 269–297.

Jackall, R. (1988). *Moral mazes* (Vol. 4). Oxford University Press.

Kotter, J. P. (1995). Leading change. *Harvard Business Review, 73*(2), 59–67.

March, H. A., & Simon, J. G. (1993). *Organizations* (2nd ed.). Blackwell.

Micklethwait, J., & Wooldridge, A. (1996). *The Witch Doctors: Making Sense of the Management Gurus.* Times Books.

Poulfelt, F. (1997). Ethics for management consultants. *Business Ethics: A European Review, 6*(2), 65–70.

Skovgaard-Smith, I. (2008). *Management consulting in action: Value creation and ambiguity in client-consultant relations.* Copenhagen Business School (CBS).

Stiglitz, J.E. (1998). Knowledge for development: Economic science, economic policy, and economic advice. In *Annual World Bank conference on development economics* (Vol. 20, pp. 9–58). World Bank.

Sturdy, A. (1997). The consultancy process: An insecure business? *Journal of Management Studies, 34*(3), 389–413.

Suddaby, R. (2006). From the editors: What grounded theory is not. *Academy of Management Journal, 49*(4), 633–642.

Veatch, T. C. (1998). A theory of humor. *Humor-International Journal of Humor Research, 11*(2), 161–216.

Open Access This chapter is licensed under the terms of the Creative Commons Attribution 4.0 International License (http://creativecommons.org/licenses/by/4.0/), which permits use, sharing, adaptation, distribution and reproduction in any medium or format, as long as you give appropriate credit to the original author(s) and the source, provide a link to the Creative Commons license and indicate if changes were made.

The images or other third party material in this chapter are included in the chapter's Creative Commons license, unless indicated otherwise in a credit line to the material. If material is not included in the chapter's Creative Commons license and your intended use is not permitted by statutory regulation or exceeds the permitted use, you will need to obtain permission directly from the copyright holder.

Chapter 6
Concluding Reflections on Jokes-Based Research Methods

6.1 Introduction

Based on the concluding sections in the previous chapters we can say that each of the applied jokes-based research methods has different strengths compared to traditional research methods in business ethics. Also compared to journalistic research, jokes-based research methods in ethics have as a strength that they uncover the more common, every day transgressions in business we feel ashamed of, and that cause strong enough emotional responses for laughing. Journalist in contrast operate more in the emotional anger zone by reporting on big scandals and major crimes.

Still, when doing research based on new jokes-based research methods, reviewers may not be familiar with their strengths. Rejection is a safe way out for them, to prevent they might suggest acceptance of an article that is flawed in its methods. The only way to convince reviewers in social science journals is to be very transparent about a new method. Transparency might be as important when submitting to philosophy journals, as they may have less tradition in publishing empirical research. In all cases it is good to describe new methods in a way that they can be replicated, and to highlight limitations carefully and explain how you have dealt with them as suggested in Suddaby (2006). That gives reviewers the best opportunities to assess a new qualitative method, or a new application.

This chapter seeks to compare the four research methods for their strength, scope and validity. The question is *when to use each of the jokes-based research methods, and for what type of ethical research questions.* While each individual method chapter has discussed strengths and weaknesses of the methods, the following sections will compare and relate scope and benefits of the four jokes-based research methods. Then, validity issues related to the methods will be discussed. Next, wider applications of the methods beyond the field of business ethics are considered, and the chapter concludes with a reflection on the normative and analytical characteristics of business jokes.

6.2 Scope and Benefits of Jokes-Based Research Methods

The four jokes-based research methods all have a different scope, ranging from narrow to broad, and they help to answer different research questions. They also have specific benefits when compared to their traditional counterparts. Table 6.1 summarizes scope and benefits of the four methods. Each method will be discussed in turn.

6.2.1 Use of Jokes as Illustration in Business Ethics Research

The scope of the first method used for illustrating empirical or theoretical arguments in business ethics is rather broad. Critical business jokes do cover the main types of

Table 6.1 Scope and benefits of jokes-based research methods

Method	Scope	Benefits
Jokes-based illustrations added (descriptive and evaluative questions)	Broad scope, common issues • Not the most recent issues • Not the most painful issues • The illustration implies valuation, abstraction, and requires interpretation	Compared to case illustrations in newspapers on business ethics: • More common transgressions • Less extreme transgressions
Jokes-based interview study (explorative questions)	Somewhat narrow scope due to interview focus • Great descriptive depth • Room for exploring memories of work experiences associated with the jokes • Interpretative reflections triggered, both normative and explanatory	Compared to traditional interviews: • More rapport • Reduced social desirability bias • Interviewee gets better access to own memories of relevant experiences
Jokes-based survey questions added (descriptive questions)	Narrow scope, linked to interpreting specific joke content • No room to go beyond the joke • Comparisons of stakeholder opinions • Part of mixed method survey design	Compared to traditional surveys: • Higher completion and response rates • Respondents get better access to own memories of relevant experiences • Visualization (cartoons) • Extra control
Jokes-based content analysis (explorative questions)	Potentially broad scope, but dependent on the sample criteria • Not the most recent issues • Not the most painful issues	Compared to common theoretical reviews in business ethics: • More empirical detail • Multiple stakeholder perspectives

unethical behaviour in the context of management consulting as explored in over 100 interviews leading to a top ten of ethical transgressions. Each one of them could be illustrated. We can expect this applies to business jokes in other fields as well, like banking, law, engineering etc. where business jokes abound. Jokes as illustration contribute to descriptive research questions that investigate various transgressions in the business world, and they help to evaluate such practices by activating shared ethical standards.

Newer kinds of transgressions were not included in jokes and cartoons in as much detail as older ones. For instance, related to new privacy rules Internet jokes or cartoons need some time to develop. With such new norms and regulations, jokes might start as workplace humour, just between colleagues, and later develop into published and shared internet jokes.

In comparison to journalistic accounts of cases based on interviews and observation, illustrative jokes and especially cartoons give less detail about how practices develop over time, what aspects have influenced a transgression, what actors were involved etc. Jokes may only highlight some relevant details, maybe exaggerate elements, use irony, leave much implicit, etc. Jokes assume the audience can fill in the gaps with experience, and is able to interpret.

In newspapers, cartoons are often published next to articles, indicating these genres can complement each other. Business jokes focus on common transgressions and can add emphasis in a business ethical argument, which may help to make a problem more visible, and mark it as a problem, to raise awareness for the illustrated norm violation. Academic articles in different fields and for different subjects have used jokes and cartoons as illustration before (i.e. Fincham, 1999, p. 341; Schneider & Sting, 2020; Sturdy et al., 2008, p. 134), but here not explicitly linked to business ethics.

6.2.2 Use of Jokes-Based Interviews in Business Ethics Research

The scope of jokes-based interview studies is more focussed than the jokes-based illustration method. Every common transgression joked about can be illustrated, whereas the topic for an interview needs some more focus. The method uses a small sample of jokes on one topic as starting point for an open in-depth interview conversation. Jokes-based interviews start with text jokes or cartoons as invitation for a conversation, and then give interviewees room to interpret and compare with their own experiences. The initial response can be denial or acceptance of a joke, but qualifications always follow, such as "true, but it is an exception". The next step is to ask for illustrations, and to discuss own experiences and similar events the respondents have witnessed. Maybe respondents can even share related workplace jokes themselves. Experiences that come to mind this way are triggered by the jokes based on associative connections. It also helps interviewees to get access to more memories. This makes the method suitable for answering open, explorative research questions.

The strength of the method is that jokes invite respondents to open up. Direct questioning about unethical behaviours mostly generates defensive responses, due to social desirability bias. Social desirability bias can be reduced when starting the conversation on ethical transgression with illustrative jokes. In my ethics classes where students need to do an interview with consultants on experienced unethical behaviours, I advise them to select some relevant cartoons to illustrate typical unethical behaviours in consulting. Students who follow up on this advice hand in interview transcripts that are in general much richer in describing events, providing more short cases and better narratives. Compared to normal interviewing the method generates richer empirical material to reflect on theoretically.

As sample sizes are limited in most interview studies, only tentative conclusions can be drawn by looking at patterns in the data. In addition, not all possible transgressions are illustrated in jokes and cartoons due to humour bias (not everything is funny). Therefore, the interviewer should be open to move away with the interviewee from the more stereotypical examples illustrated in jokes, memes and cartoons. It is good practice to explore the more common and stereotypical examples first, relate them to experiences of the interviewee as familiar or not, and then move on to more nuanced, deeper and related experiences later in the interview, when trust has been established, and the taboo character of the topic has become less salient.

6.2.3 Use of Jokes-Based Surveys in Business Ethics Research

The third method based on a jokes-based survey with rating questions can only assess the content given in the presented cartoons. That makes the scope of the method rather narrow. There is no room to go beyond the cartoon as in open interviews. Therefore it important to carefully select a set of relevant cartoons related to the issue. That the cartoons have a focus on common and stereotypical transgressions is no disadvantage, because larger groups of respondents will be able to give their opinion related to the criticisms, as they are relatively well known. The method picks up on the fact that different respondents have different perspectives towards the ethics claims made in business jokes. When rating cartoons in a survey, it is possible to compare average stakeholder responses for groups. That makes the method suitable to answer descriptive research questions, and to quantify, rate and compare.

A challenge is to identify the different respondent groups. If stakeholder groups can be identified, based on some diagnostic questions, follow-up questions can be about perceptions of funniness, truth elements and specific characteristics of the presented cartoons. Cartoons are more suitable in a survey than text jokes, due to their visual communication and fast transmission of the message. The less time a survey takes, the better for response and completion rates.

Integrating jokes in survey questions improves response rates and completion rates due to the fun aspect of doing the survey. The cartoons also stimulate the mind and give better access to memories as observed with jokes-based interviews. As an additional type of questions, they can serve as control questions.

6.2.4 Use of Jokes-Based Content Analysis in Business Ethics Research

The fourth method is most dependent on the content provided in jokes such as cartoons, memes or other humorous sources that are analysed. As with the illustration method the scope is potentially broad, but limited by the sample criteria. In contrast to the third approach, all relevant jokes related to the topic found online can be included in the sample. With a larger set of jokes more ethical aspects can be joked about, and more content is available for content analysis.

The method of jokes-based content analysis fits explorative research questions. For exploring a relatively nascent empirical field of research in business ethics, content analysis of critical business jokes can generate relevant new insights, covering multiple stakeholder perspectives and adding more detail and nuance to earlier findings in academic literature, as shown in the example study.

Jokes-based content analysis is a promising approach in the context of business ethics, related to various themes and professions, when research is nascent and questions are explorative. Limitations of the method are that jokes might not cover the most recent ethical issues, and not the most serious ones, but only the more common transgressions that meet the normality condition. Compared to traditional philosophical studies in business ethics the method can provide more empirical detail on the more common transgressions, and on the kind of ethical standards that are violated in business contexts.

6.3 Validity of the Four Jokes-Based Research Methods

If the validity of a method improves, research findings and conclusions become more truthful, credible and accurate. When doing qualitative research, criteria to realize this are different from criteria for quantitative research (Golafshani, 2003). Qualitative research has a focus on words in "observation, interviews, extracts from documents, [and] tape recordings" (Miles & Huberman, 1984, p. 23). Words express subjective experiences, meanings, social context and a researcher aims at intersubjective validity of interpretations. The four jokes-based research methods are all based on words, image and interpretation. That has impact on what potential kinds of bias need attention, to improve reliability and validity of results and conclusions.

Table 6.2 Validity issues related to jokes-based research methods

Jokes-based methods and impacted validity conditions	Illustration	Interview	Survey	Content analysis
Importance context knowledge researchers (for interpretation)	+	+	++	++
Importance topical fit (data selection)	++	+	++	+
Dependence on the jokes' content (data quality; humour bias)	+	+	++	++
Importance sample size of jokes (data quality; neutralizing representation bias)	+	+	+	++
Possibilities for triangulation (data analysis)	++	++	++	+
Reduced social desirability bias (data quality)		++	+	
Importance context knowledge respondents (for interpretation)		+	++	
Importance context knowledge readers (for interpretation)	+	+	+	++

Improving reliability means that other researchers doing the same research in a comparable research context will come to similar conclusions (Brink, 1993; Bryman, 2016; Miles & Huberman, 1984). Therefore researchers should describe exactly what they did: how they sampled, collected and analysed data, etc. They make their method transparent and replicable. To further improve validity, several practices have been suggested, focusing on possible bias that relates to the researcher, the data and their analysis, the study participants (respondents), and the audience (Brink, 1993; Creswell & Miller, 2000; Gioia et al., 2013; Miles & Huberman, 1984). For each of the four jokes-based methods potential biases and validity conditions work out differently. Table 6.2 summarizes these differences, where + indicates importance/dependence etc. and ++ great importance/dependence etc. of the validity condition for the method. The conditions will be discussed in turn.

Starting with the researcher, interpretive abilities need to be excellent (Alvesson, 2003; Brink, 1993; Creswell & Miller, 2000; Miles & Huberman, 1984). In the jokes-based illustration method, selection of illustrative jokes is dependent on researcher interpretation. A check with the audience is important, to see if the selected illustration also makes sense to others. This happens automatically in the second and third method when respondents interpret jokes. It gives researchers access to different interpretative perspectives next to their own. When reporting results it is important to distinguish in the presentation between respondents interpretation of jokes, and when respondents contrast interpretations with their own experiences. In illustrative quotes readers should also be able to see these differences. There are also other ways to reduce researcher bias when doing jokes-based content analysis: by doing the interpretation in steps, asking friendly reviewers to look at the work, and relating codes to what we know already from earlier research. A recommended approach is

6.3 Validity of the Four Jokes-Based Research Methods

also to do interpretations with two or more researchers independently, and discuss different interpretations to improve intercoder reliability (Gioia et al., 2013, p. 22). For all methods it is important to be reflective on the researcher in the research process.

A second source of potential bias for jokes-based research approaches are the data and their analysis: jokes can be seen as biased data, and like metaphors not always easy to understand (Cornelissen & Kafouros, 2008). In several ways they are more biased than the stories respondents may tell in interviews. The good thing is that we *know* that jokes carry fiction, abstraction, irony, exaggeration, distortion, stereotypes, etc. A joke signals this, which makes the interpreter alert. In contrast, a lie or an inaccurate memory reported in an interview does not. A good way to filter out fact from fiction is data triangulation. In the first method: compare the jokes-based illustration carefully with the reported transgression; in the second method: compare the presented illustrative jokes carefully with the interpretations and experiences shared by interviewees; in the third method: carefully compare results from the mixed method survey approach; with the method of jokes-based content analysis: make the sample size big enough by doing extensive internet searches that the sample allows for data triangulation. While fictional elements may vary a lot between jokes on the same topic, the factual elements may present a pattern. The better a transgression is grounded in various jokes, the stronger the pattern and the more valid the basis for interpretation. Existing studies on the topic can also be a point of reference for interpreting the jokes, next to context knowledge and relevant experiences interpreters possess. Jokes are not only biased, as stated before they are also limited in their scope. They only represent common, stereotypical, middle of the road ethical transgressions that can be joked about. To avoid that jokes may have a leading influence on what people say in jokes-based interviews, it is important to let the conversation move towards respondents' own experiences after a while by asking follow-up questions. To reduce bias related to the messages carried by the selected illustrative jokes in interview settings, respondents can also be asked to choose from more jokes, which is similar to working with a more open topic list (cf. Hermanowicz, 2002). In both the second and third method it is also important to make clear the jokes do not represent the researchers', but a public opinion.

A third source of bias relates to study participants, as noted in the second and third method. We have discussed this as social desirability or memory bias. Participants sometimes just don't remember or cannot tell. Here the jokes were of great value to reduce this bias by creating better rapport, a safer space to talk about ethical transgressions, and also as a trigger for memories. As respondents are involved in joke interpretation, context knowledge on their side is important to. With interviews respondents are selected for their context knowledge, and this can be checked during the interview. For survey respondents this check is more difficult to realize, but some diagnostic questions may be added for this purpose.

A fourth source of bias might come from audiences like reviewers and readers (Creswell & Miller, 2000). Especially with jokes-based content analysis, the audience that reads the results of an content analysis needs sufficient context knowledge to be able to follow the interpretation of the researchers. Not all audiences might be able to. One solution is to target the right audience via the journal you want to publish in. Another option is to provide sufficient context when introducing a joke, much like the way I do in Chap. 2. Here jokes are illustrating interviewee experiences that were shared first, to provide some context knowledge. How serious the audience problem can be is illustrated by my teaching experiences with fresh students in the MSc management consulting at Vrije Universiteit Amsterdam. When I confront them with consultant jokes in the first weeks of the program, mostly none out of a group of 50 or more students is able to provide a reasonable interpretation. They come up with a lot of ideas and associations, but they just miss the context knowledge needed to interpret the joke well.

6.4 Wider Applications of Jokes-Based Research Methods

6.4.1 Using Jokes-Based Research Methods in Wider Contexts of Norm Violation

The four jokes-based research methods discussed here are developed in the context of management consulting, with a focus on ethical transgressions. The method can also be applied in other business contexts where actors behave unethically. Other professions under humorous attack are lawyers with many published jokes expressing unethical lawyer practices (Galanter, 1997), and there are many jokes about politicians (Benson, 2020; Lukes & Galnoor, 1985; Wilde, 1984), bankers (Young, 2011), etc.

Jokes-based research methods are not only useful in contexts where common transgressions are ethical, but also in contexts were other norms or traditions are mildly violated as with technological innovations that go beyond our comfort zone, with new fashions where people cannot keep up, with foreign, old or new traditions, or other common developments that may feel emotionally absurd. Joking extends into various domains of life, and may provide valuable data on the illustrated and recognizable norm transgressions.

6.4.2 Jokes-Based Research in Course Assignments

Apart from application in academic research, jokes-based research methods can be applied in courses on business ethics that prepare students for a professional role as teacher, doctor, nurse, banker, lawyer, manager, consultant etc. When students prepare for a professional role, it is very educational to study the ethical challenges in the profession based on newspaper cases, but in addition also based on content analysis of humorous accounts. Next, students can move to having a conversation with professionals in the field, using the jokes-based interview method. What are the real-life challenges these professionals experience? Is it part of daily life, or are these more incidental challenges? Are there ways out? The position of a novice to the profession may create some goodwill, and starting a conversation with some jokes on the profession will add to breaking the ice.

Without sharing some jokes during a conversation on ethical challenges in the work life of consultants, many of my students have met defensive professionals who explain what great measures there are in place to prevent unethical practices from happening at all, and how well organised their professional practice is. A way to prevent such defensive conversations is the use of humour, thus creating a critical outsider (the cartoonist, the anonymous joke author), and reflect on the context or situation referred to in such a joke, and then start the conversation. Interviewees may get better access to their relevant memories and experiences this way, and feel less in need to defend their own ethical position. Jokes help to create a play frame, and make the issue less threatening, which may further reduce social desirability pressures (Sturdy et al., 2008).

6.4.3 Further Sources to Explore in Jokes-Based Research Methods

Text jokes and cartoons are not the only humorous genres. There are humorous pictures, short videos, longer films, series, plays, etc. Jokes have an advantage over other genres that they are very concise, especially cartoons. That makes that they can easily be integrated in an interview or survey, as reading them does not consume much time. Still, other humorous genres might also offer good material for ethical reflection. Genres that might fulfil this role are comical plays, movies, TV series, recorded acts of comedians, comics or humorous novels and stories.

How these other genres could be used needs to be tried. When time to read or watch them is limited, one option is selecting quotes: text quotes, video quotes and other short extracts. Context knowledge based on earlier scenes in a story or movie is missing then, so it should be possible to provide the audience with sufficient background knowledge. Especially with TV series, much pre knowledge is assumed, so this might not always be possible. Maybe sub narratives within a larger story can be used. Short videos might also focus on relevant themes like unequal gender relations, diversity issues, problematic manager-employee or consultant-client relations etc. See for instance this short and funny YouTube video on ethics in a publisher-author relationship: https://youtu.be/dx71U3u--qU.

There would be a few novels on consultants to explore, and there is a well-known TV series called *House of Lies* based on a novel by Kihn (2012). On marketing advisers there is the famous series *Mad Man*. Elements of the North American business culture and business ethics of the 1960s can be found here, whereas House of Lies refers to business culture and ethics 50 years later, showing many similarities but also differences in the illustrated ethical transgressions.

In three of the discussed methods there is a serious time or space limit for the humorous genre to be used (jokes-based illustration, interview, survey). However, for content analysis there is no such strict time limit. Humorous TV series, novels and plays may then offer rich materials for content analysis. The downside may be that background research done by novelists, movie makers and comic writers is usually not of the same quality as the studies of business historians or journalists. As with jokes, what they present does not need to be true due to fictional elements. Some more sources need to be used at least. Still, the work of Nussbaum (1995, 2001) is inspirational here.

The potential in terms of data on ethical (mal)practice in novels, plays, movies, series etc. is substantial, especially related to more long standing professions. While consultants have a relatively low representation in these literary genres, judges, lawyers, medical specialists, nurses, teachers, police officers, managers, soldiers and other economic or political characters are all much better represented in these genres, with more possibilities for content analysis related to their ethics.

6.5 Analytic and Normative Value of Jokes in Business Ethics

Humour theory as articulated by Veatch (1998) has indicated how two conditions simultaneously apply to various expressions of humour. Expressions of humour can be text jokes, cartoons, memes but also comedy, and daily forms of humour that develop between colleagues, between friends etc. The normality criterion explains why ethical transgressions referred to in critical business jokes should be common enough to be recognizable for audiences familiar with the context. The condition of emotional absurdity due to mild norm violation helps to explain why humour is able to express moral criticism. Critical business jokes that survive on the Internet or get shared elsewhere, must meet both conditions.

The normality condition indicates why jokes can become the eyes and ears of business ethics. Business jokes address ethical transgressions that happen, that those who laugh can recognize. Jokes that do not refer to what happens in reality, lack funniness or might be considered an insinuation. However, as soon as audiences recognize a joke's truth and start laughing, they admit they know what is meant. The normality condition guarantees that popular business jokes cover something real, which gives them diagnostic qualities. Therefore, business jokes can help the scholar in business ethics to identify what ethical transgressions happen in the field.

The condition that requires mild norm violation and feelings of emotional absurdity enables the bridge from humour to ethics as topic. As emotional absurdity is triggered by a mild offense of norms, principles or common expectations, common ethical transgressions are fitting the second condition. Business jokes can draw on ethical transgressions that are experienced as emotionally absurd or unexpected. Ethical transgressions are very popular joking material, next to situations that are seen as ugly or out of fashion (aesthetic transgressions), behaving foolishly or impractical and other common ways of stepping out of line. As McGraw and Warren (2010) have confirmed empirically, humour flourishes especially in the grey zone of benign violations in ethics, where norm violation is mild as argued by Veatch (1998) and transgressions are not too extreme. Still, what is seen as funny in a business context, can already feel extreme and less funny for outsiders with more ambitious moral standards (cf. Carr, 1968). However, by framing moral transgressions in a business context as humorous in an interview or survey, it may help to lower the pressures of social desirability bias. Jokes frame them implicitly as benign violations, which may help respondents to open up.

Using critical business jokes in research on ethical transgressions has the potential to bridge positive research traditions in moral psychology and normative traditions in philosophical ethics. Psychologist study for instance moral disengagement; bystander effects and demoralizing effects of social systems (Alzola, 2008; O'Mahoney, 2011; Schaefer & Bouwmeester, 2021), while philosophical studies on normative ethics refer to moral intuitions, moral emotions and normative principles (Ten Bos & Willmott, 2001). Due to the two humour conditions jokes relate to both this positive and normative tradition: they assess behaviours as unethical, as well as that they illustrate such common behaviours and describe key characteristics. Jokes can thus illustrate and support theoretical arguments that go in normative directions by articulating absurdities, as well as illustrate empirical claims about unethical behaviours as being common and recognizable practices. Jokes thus powerfully integrate positive and normative content. Both content elements can be analysed via jokes-based content analysis or discussed in jokes-based interviews. Similarly, both sides of jokes can be reflected on in surveys.

Using jokes-based research methods in business ethics may also create bridges between predominantly positivist and more engaged or critical research traditions that are coexisting in moral psychology, several social sciences, critical management studies and business ethics. Whereas psychologists mostly study individual level behaviours, social scientists also study the influence of social systems on ethical behaviour, as well as organisational level actions and responsibilities. Business jokes discuss such interactions, and illustrate how the individual, their scripted roles and the wider social context influence each other. By illustrating such interactions business jokes exploit several kinds of emotional absurdities, like meeting system demands at the cost of personal work-life balance (which is made fun of), or creating a very profitable business practice at the expense of moral leadership (which is made fun of), etc. In addition, there are bridges to methods of the humanities. Various narrative methods have found their way into the social sciences already (cf. Czarniawska, 1997). Jokes-based research methods could be added to this project. Not only can wider social critiques be expressed in jokes and thus analysed this way, business ethics scholars may also invest in jokes-based research methods to study organisation level or occupational phenomena. Humour then may have a liberating effect, for instance by loosening the pressure of giving social desirable answers in interviews. This property of freeing up the mind is what Watson (2015) values, when advocating the use of humour and irony in social science research.

Finally, joking can be seen as an art. Cartoonists will consider themselves artists for sure, given the visual expression and their artistic signature. Jokes mostly are collective art, including many anonymous artists, showing gradual development and travel between outlets and audiences. It is not considered museum art, or high standing literature such as poems, but still a form of artwork with elements of emphasis and expression. Although being a work of art, jokes can bridge towards science by their strong diagnostic qualities. Like science has many implied normative elements, for instance by the selection of what is studied and what not, critical business jokes appear to be very accurate in illustrating common processes and practices that society would assess as immoral. These characteristics make jokes powerful in business ethics as illustrations of an empirical or theoretical argument, very motivational as triggers in an interview conversation, very clear and pronounced as statements to assess in a survey, and very rich as data sources for interpretative content analysis.

References

Alvesson, M. (2003). Beyond neopositivists, romantics, and localists: A reflexive approach to interviews in organizational research. *Academy of Management Review, 28*(1), 13–33.
Alzola, M. (2008). Character and environment: The status of virtues in organizations. *Journal of Business Ethics, 78*(3), 343–357.
Benson, T. (2020). *Britain's best political cartoons*. Penguin.
Brink, H. I. (1993). Validity and reliability in qualitative research. *Curationis, 16*(2), 35–38.
Bryman, A. (2016). *Social research methods*. Oxford University Press.
Carr, A. Z. (1968). Is business bluffing ethical. *Harvard Business Review, 46*(1), 143–153.
Cornelissen, J. P., & Kafouros, M. (2008). Metaphors and theory building in organization theory: What determines the impact of a metaphor on theory? *British Journal of Management, 19*(4), 365–379.
Creswell, J. W., & Miller, D. L. (2000). Determining validity in qualitative inquiry. *Theory into Practice, 39*(3), 124–130.
Czarniawska, B. (1997). *A narrative approach to organization studies*. Sage Publications.
Fincham, R. (1999) The Consultant-Client Relationship: Critical Perspectives on the Management of Organizational Change. *Journal of Management Studies, 36*(3) 335–351. https://doi.org/10.1111/1467-6486.00139
Galanter, M. (1997). The faces of mistrust: The image of lawyers in public opinion, jokes, and political discourse. *University of Cincinatti Law Review, 66*(3), 805–845.
Gioia, D. A., Corley, K. G., & Hamilton, A. L. (2013). Seeking qualitative rigor in inductive research: Notes on the Gioia methodology. *Organizational Research Methods, 16*(1), 15–31.
Golafshani, N. (2003). Understanding reliability and validity in qualitative research. *The Qualitative Report, 8*(4), 597–607.
Hermanowicz, J. C. (2002). The great interview: 25 strategies for studying people in bed. *Qualitative Sociology, 25*(4), 479–499.
Kihn, M. (2012). *House of lies: How management consultants steel your watch and then tell you the time*. Business Plus.
Lukes, S., & Galnoor, I. (1985). *No laughing matter: A collection of political jokes*. Routledge.
McGraw, A. P., & Warren, C. (2010). Benign violations: Making immoral behavior funny. *Psychological Science, 21*(8), 1141–1149.

References

Miles, M. B., & Huberman, A. M. (1984). Drawing valid meaning from qualitative data: Toward a shared craft. *Educational Researcher, 13*(5), 20–30.

Nussbaum, M. (1995). *Poetic justice: The literary imagination and public life*. Beacon Press.

Nussbaum, M. C. (2001). *The fragility of goodness: Luck and ethics in Greek tragedy and philosophy*. Cambridge University Press.

O'Mahoney, J. (2011). Advisory anxieties: Ethical individualisation in the UK consulting industry. *Journal of Business Ethics, 104*(1), 101–113.

Schaefer, U., & Bouwmeester, O. (2021). Reconceptualizing moral disengagement as a process: Transcending overly liberal and overly conservative practice in the field. *Journal of Business Ethics, 172*(3), 525–543. https://doi.org/10.1007/s10551-020-04520-6

Schneider, P., & Sting, F. J. (2020). Employees' perspectives on digitalization-induced change: Exploring frames of industry 4.0. *Academy of Management Discoveries, 6*(3), 406–435.

Sturdy, A., Clark, T., Fincham, R., & Handley, K. (2008). Management consultancy and humor in action and context. In S. Fineman (Ed.), *The emotional organization: Passions and power* (pp. 134–150). Blackwell.

Suddaby, R. (2006). *From the editors: What grounded theory is not*. Academy of Management

Ten Bos, R., & Willmott, H. (2001). Towards a post-dualistic business ethics: Interweaving reason and emotion in working life. *Journal of Management Studies, 38*(6), 769–793.

Veatch, T. C. (1998). A theory of humor. *Humor-International Journal of Humor Research, 11*(2), 161–216.

Watson, C. (2015). *Comedy and social science: Towards a methodology of funny*. Routledge.

Wilde, L. (1984). *The official politicians joke book*. Bantam Books.

Young, M. G. (2011). *The best ever book of banker jokes: Lots and lots of jokes specially repur-posed for you-know-who*. CreateSpace Independent Publishing Platform.

Open Access This chapter is licensed under the terms of the Creative Commons Attribution 4.0 International License (http://creativecommons.org/licenses/by/4.0/), which permits use, sharing, adaptation, distribution and reproduction in any medium or format, as long as you give appropriate credit to the original author(s) and the source, provide a link to the Creative Commons license and indicate if changes were made.

The images or other third party material in this chapter are included in the chapter's Creative Commons license, unless indicated otherwise in a credit line to the material. If material is not included in the chapter's Creative Commons license and your intended use is not permitted by statutory regulation or exceeds the permitted use, you will need to obtain permission directly from the copyright holder.

GPSR Compliance

The European Union's (EU) General Product Safety Regulation (GPSR) is a set of rules that requires consumer products to be safe and our obligations to ensure this.

If you have any concerns about our products, you can contact us on

ProductSafety@springernature.com

In case Publisher is established outside the EU, the EU authorized representative is:

Springer Nature Customer Service Center GmbH
Europaplatz 3
69115 Heidelberg, Germany

www.ingramcontent.com/pod-product-compliance
Ingram Content Group UK Ltd.
Pitfield, Milton Keynes, MK11 3LW, UK
UKHW021041050925
462611UK00011B/979